MW00447816

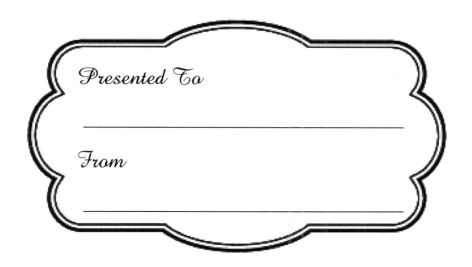

Presented To

_____

From

_____

HOW TO BUILD A SPORT OR LIFE DYNASTY

By
Norbert A. Baschnagel
Retired Full Professor, Clarion University of PA

DORRANCE
PUBLISHING CO
EST. 1920
PITTSBURGH, PENNSYLVANIA 15238

The contents of this work, including, but not limited to, the accuracy of events, people, and places depicted; opinions expressed; permission to use previously published materials included; and any advice given or actions advocated are solely the responsibility of the author, who assumes all liability for said work and indemnifies the publisher against any claims stemming from publication of the work.

All Rights Reserved
Copyright © 2021 by Norbert A. Baschnagel

No part of this book may be reproduced or transmitted, downloaded, distributed, reverse engineered, or stored in or introduced into any information storage and retrieval system, in any form or by any means, including photocopying and recording, whether electronic or mechanical, now known or hereinafter invented without permission in writing from the publisher.

Dorrance Publishing Co
585 Alpha Drive
Pittsburgh, PA 15238
Visit our website at *www.dorrancebookstore.com*

ISBN: 978-1-6495-7242-4
eISBN: 978-1-6495-7750-4

CONTENTS

- Dynasty's Research
- Norb Baschnagel's Triangle To Success
- Success to Significance – Serve Your Community
- Community Fundraising
- Community Service Awards

OPENING STATEMENT

My goal is of vital importance to me that you clearly understand who I am. My whole life philosophy is based on four words, "Give me your best." This philosophy is very simple and it is very hard to uphold all of the time.

Give me your best will help you to attain success. Attaining success is very complicated and extremely difficult. That's why I've chosen and discuss ten (10) leadership qualities that I believe are most important to help one attain success: sportsmanship, caring, persistence, hard work, enthusiasm, skill, conditioning, discipline, teamwork, and friendship. These leadership qualities make up my "Triangle to Success." I strongly feel you need these qualities to develop your own sport or life dynasty.

Seek success with all you've got, and you'll do just fine. Teach the same to those in your organization or team, and they too will have the tools necessary to achieve greatness. That's my promise to you. I can make that promise because that's exactly the way I did it to create a tennis sport and life dynasty at Clarion University and in the Clarion Community.

I try very hard not to play politics and to be honest, show sportsmanship, and do the best for my church, family, university, and the community. I believe that if you want to be happy for a lifetime you must volunteer and help someone. I also believe that if you want to be happy for a lifetime you must be a giver and a steward for your community. This book, *How to Build a Sport or Life Dynasty,* is a book about how important it is to have a positive attitude: "The greatest discovery of any generation is that a human being can alter his life by altering his/her attitude" (William James).

A dynasty in sports is a team that dominates or excels among their division, league, and/or sport over an extended period of time, such as multiple seasons or years. Dynasties are usually realized after the fact in retrospect or during the fact after an established period of dominance.

This book, I believe, will be a success because every coach in the country, at all levels, wants to build their own sport or life dynasty. We built a sport dynasty in Women's Tennis at Clarion University with very little scholarship aid and very little tennis budget. To my knowledge, no other sport in the history of Clarion University has accomplished the goals we did with very little scholarship aid. I know this book will help others attain success because I didn't play high school or college tennis, and I am a much better basketball coach than tennis coach, but, because I practiced the leadership qualities I outlined in the book, I was able to build a sport and life dynasty. I believe anyone can develop their own sport or life dynasty if they follow my recommendations. I believe that ninety percent (90%) of your success in life has to do with having a positive attitude and you must believe in yourself, have the confidence, and leadership qualities of sportsmanship, caring, persistence, discipline, dedication, hard work, teamwork, conditioning, friendship, and the skills sets needed to accomplish all your goals.

"Within you right now is the power to do things you never dreamed possible. This power becomes available to you as soon as you change your attitude" (Maxwell Maltz).

FAITH, FAMILY, AND FRIENDS

While this book is about my Tennis Dynasty, I find that tennis, like virtually everything in life, does not stand alone, but is caught up in a web that connects it to many other parts of our lives - our goals, our dreams, our faith, and our families. In my own case, I found, while writing this book about my successful career in tennis, that my career was shaped by more than just the technical knowledge of the game. It was also shaped by the things I value and love the most Faith, Family, and Friends.

FAITH: Faith in God is the source of one's ethics, morality, character, leadership, courtesy, sense of fairness, honesty, integrity, caring, trust, compassion, responsibility, respect and all the other qualities that go into making for good sportsmanship in tennis and life. I encourage all my student-athletes to draw on their own faith to develop these values, just as I do.

FAMILY: My family is literally the ground of my being on this earth: they support me, encourage me, cheer me on, and love me without question. This book is dedicated to my wife Beverly Jane Hey Baschnagel who is the best thing that has ever happened to me and is the love of my life.

Dedication

This book is dedicated to my wife Beverly. All of my great accolades, statements, awards, and accomplishments could not have been possible without my wife, who is the "Love of my life" and who has given me the greatest gift of all, her love and the opportunity to share our lives together for the past forty-five (45) years. Bev, you are the best thing that has ever happened to me. You have changed my life for the better, and no dream of tomorrow would be complete without you there by my side. Without your loyalty, trust, persistent encouragement, honesty, inspiration, support, caring, and love for me, I would not have accomplished anything.

Thank you for your patience, love, and understanding me for all these years. Our family is blessed because you have been the spiritual and moral rock for me and our children. I am grateful for all you do to make a loving home for our family. They are very lucky and blessed to have you as their mother and grandmother.

You have stuck by me in good times and bad times; you put up with my faults and still love me in spite of them. I apologize for my faults and bad times. You have made my life full, and I thank you for all the very happy days and vacations we shared as a couple and family. Most important, I've learned that I have all I'll ever need in life, because I have you, the one I love more than anyone.

You have been the work horse of our family and have carried everyone in our family and me. You have backed me for all these years and let me do it "My Way". I can never thank you enough for your loyalty and love. You are the most honest and trustworthy person I know and I thank you for taking care of me for all these years. You have eye problems but you never complain and just get the work done. You bring so much joy to my life just by being the beautiful, caring person you are. I am a very lucky man to be your husband. "I Love you" are just three words, but when I say them, I'm telling you that you're my comfort, my laughter, and my closest friend in the world. Thank you for making my life fantastic and giving me your love.

Love,
Norb

Family Continued:
In addition to my wife, whom I dedicated this book to, there are seven (7) other family members whom I would like to single out who had a direct impact on my life and on my basketball playing, teaching, coaching, and tennis coaching, and giving careers to my community. Below, I have acknowledged my brother and my six (6) children from oldest to youngest.

Charles E. Baschnagel: My brother, who is five years older than me, was five inches taller than me when he was my first basketball coach when I was in elementary school at Holy Name of Jesus Elementary School. He beat me in 100 straight games of one-on-one basketball competition. From those games, Charles taught me the meaning of sportsmanship, competitive greatness, fight, intensity, persistence, concentration, and the need to continue to work hard and focus on your objective, and never to give-up until you reach your goal. When I finally beat my brother in one-on-one basketball competition, he never beat me again, and he helped me dominate my own age level of basketball competition. He was very instrumental in helping me receive a full athletic basketball scholarship at the University of Buffalo. Chuck and I fought almost every day when we were growing up, but now we are the best of friends. Having a brother means that when you need a friend, you never have to look further than your own family. When there's someone in your life who's made a difference, whose loyalty and friendship have been yours as long as you can remember, and who's shared good times and memories with you, it's a gift you really cherish. He is a wonderful friend. I believe that if my brother did not teach me to be humble and also help me develop my sportsmanship and persistence to work hard, to reach my goals, and to dominate your opponent in sport and life, this book, *How to Build a Sport or Life Dynasty,* would not exist.

Nancy A. Baschnagel: Nancy is the eldest of my children and has taught me how to be a kind giving person and be a giver of yourself when you have very little. Nancy is an extraordinary hard worker. People really like her because she is honest, kind, and loves to help her Dementia and Alzheimer's clients. Nancy enjoys giving presents to her parents and all her brothers and sisters at Christmas time. This shows a great love and kindness to me and her family. A daughter grows up and becomes a woman, but the things you wish for her don't change at all. I wish her all the wonder of discovery, the joy of learning new things each day, a strong, steady faith to guide her, and growing confidence in her own wisdom and ability. Wherever she goes, no matter how far, I wish with all my heart that she'll always know just how much she is loved.

Robert E. Baschnagel: Robert, my eldest son, has taught me how important family is because at age three (3) he and his older sister, Nancy, were ripped away from me by my ex-wife. He is a survivor of his mother's four divorces, and four dads. Robert is a great son, excellent husband, father, brother, and provider for his remarkable family. He has a great attitude and is a good role model for his family. Bob is a very good storyteller lacing each story with much humor. I am very lucky to have such a great son. With so much love and pride, I've loved watching Bob grow up becoming the honorable giving man he is today. Bob has found his way in this world, figuring out what was right for himself. He has become a caring man and a devoted father and husband. It is so very rewarding for me to now see so many of his loving and familiar traits in his children. Saying he's made me proud would be an understatement.

Heidi Jane Baschnagel: My daughter Heidi has shown me how to show compassion for people who are having trouble in their lives. Heidi is a talented loving daughter who shares her beautiful gift of voice with others and who works very hard as a speech therapist. At the same time, she tries to help her friends have better and more enjoyable lives. Heidi has a great attitude and wants to be a friend to everyone. She is a wonderful daughter and loving person who cares about helping people. When you have a daughter who makes you proud, makes you laugh, and very often makes your day, you know what joy is. When you have a daughter whose beautiful spirit is matched by her compassion for others, you know what love is. Heidi has truly blessed my life.

Charles N. Baschnagel: My son Charles is a wonderful and intelligent man, who has a great attitude, work ethic, and talent to solve difficult problems. He has helped me to invest wisely. Charles is a remarkable son and loving and devoted husband and father who cares for and provides well for his lovely wife and adorable children each day. From the day he was born, Charles has pursued his own unique place in the world and original points of view. He is always willing to take on challenges and not settle for something just because it's easy or popular. Charles is a very good man, and with all he has to offer, he'll always be truly successful in whatever he sets his mind on. He must stay true to who he is and keep his eye on what really matters to him, and he will achieve great things for himself and others. I am so proud of him and love him so much.

Peter N. Baschnagel: My son Peter is a consistently strong, steadfast, caring, loyal, very intelligent, and thoughtful son and man. In his low key and calming ways, he has taught me how to be humble and has helped me with some medical problems over the years. He helps without fanfare but with success. Peter is also a very loving husband who works very hard providing well for his lovely wife and their dogs. There's no sweeter mystery than when holding my son as he lay fast asleep in my arms as a child and wondering what he was dreaming. I'd watch him at play as his imagination took him someplace I couldn't quite follow. I saw his interests, his tastes, and his talents taking shape. I'm so proud of the wonderful man he's grown up to be. I'm so proud to have him as my son and I love him so much.

Grace E. Baschnagel Wade: My youngest daughter Grace has taught me how to be creative and think out of the box. She is a very loving daughter, who has two beautiful children, a loving and hardworking husband, and a great creative mind who is always looking forward to improving and getting better. Grace has helped me with my two published books on how to direct successful Fun with Fundamental Basketball Camps. She is a caring and giving daughter who has been very loyal and loving. Seeing my daughter blossom into a wonderful mother is one of life's sweetest gifts. One of the greatest joys in life is watching a beautiful daughter grow up to become a warm and caring mother with children of her own, seeing family values and traditions continue, and seeing the love that holds all of us close become richer and deeper with time.

Grace will always be a wonderful and loving daughter who I love very much.

Friends:

Acknowledgments

I would like to express my sincere gratitude to the following individuals for their contributions in the making of this book, *How to Build a Sport or Life Dynasty.*

John R. Wooden: Coach Wooden was the Head Men's Basketball Coach at UCLA. He is a member of the Basketball Hall of Fame as a player and coach, who was also selected as the Coach of the Century for all sports in 2011. In my opinion, he is the greatest coach of all time. I believe, if he were coaching today, he would be as successful as he was in the past because his philosophy is based on sound principles of life and basketball fundamentals and strategies.

His "Pyramid of Success" has timeless qualities, and I have used his qualities of leadership throughout my teaching and coaching career for many years. Mr. Wooden did more than coach basketball players. He shaped the lives of thousands of people by the way he taught, wrote books, spoke, believed, acted, and interacted with people. He didn't simply teach about offense and defense with X's and O's on a chart. Coach Wooden was about sharing his values and ideals. He felt that God had given him a tremendous gift for teaching, coaching, and reaching people. He believed that "To whom much is given, much is required." Mr. Wooden was a man of dignity and integrity. I have tried to follow his principles of teaching and coaching by incorporating them into my classes, my coaching, my camps, and the books that I published. His influence is present in giving to my community and my family. I will continue to carry the mantle and carry the legacy of John Wooden.

Review of Manuscript:

Dr. William Buchanan – Full Professor Information and Library Science Department Clarion University (retired – 2019) and friend for over 20 years.

Father Samuel Bungo – Pastor of Saint Charles Church, New Bethlehem, PA, Parochial Vicar at Immaculate Conception Church in Clarion, PA, Campus Minister for Clarion State College 1981, and friend for over 38 years.

Phil Popielski - Assistant Principal at Woodlawn High School in Baltimore County Public Schools, former Women's Assistant Basketball Coach at McDaniel College, former Student Assistant Coach for the Women's Tennis Team at Clarion University (1983 to 1987), CUP Alumni 1987, and friend for over 36 year.

Tamara Myers - CUP Alumni 1991, CUP Captain of Clarion University Women's Tennis Team 1989-1990, CUP Athletic Hall of Fame Member 2011, Medical Salesperson, and friend over 33 Years.

Bonnie Wolbert – Present Athletic Director of North Clarion High School, Retired English Teacher at North Clarion High

School 33 years, 2018 Clarion County YMCA "Sportsmanship I" Sportsperson of the Year for Western Pennsylvania, and friend 26 Years.

Robert Tonkin – Former Athletic Director for 15 years at Brookville High School, 2000 Region III Athletic Director of the Year, 2019 Clarion County YMCA "Sportsmanship I" Sportsperson of the Year for Western Pennsylvania, and friend for 5 Years.

Cover Design: Scott Kane
Photographer: Whitling Photography of Clarion, PA

Women's Tennis Team Players and Student Assistant Coaches:
I would like to acknowledge and thank all my players on my tennis teams from 1982 to 1989 who helped build a Women's Tennis Team Dynasty at Clarion University of PA:

I would also like to acknowledge and thank the following student assistant coaches for my tennis teams, Phil Popielski, Sue Reeder, Debra Kotula, Sue Fritz, and Jim Bowman, who worked hard with our players to instill desire, work ethic, and improvement. They were also a real positive influence for the women's CUP tennis program. They prepared the tennis courts for practice and tennis matches; they rolled and squeegeed the courts when it rained or snowed so that we could have our practice or dual match. They helped with practice drills, assisted the athletic trainer, and also helped with recruiting players.

I also want to acknowledge and thank Dawn Funya, a former player as our publicity chairman (1986) in which her job was to make Clarion University and the Clarion community aware of the team's successes and progress.

Tennis Booster Club Founders:

I would like to thank two of my best friends, Steve Dudurich and Larry Schmader for founding the Clarion University Women's Tennis Booster Club in 1986 and helping recruit over 100 members to help supplement the financial needs for the CUP Women's Tennis Budget, raising over $10,000 from 1986 to 1990. They helped fund the season opening picnic for the tennis team, at my home and the end-of-season banquet to honor the tennis team especially gifts for the graduating seniors. They also helped upgrade the level of equipment of the Women's Tennis Team at Clarion University.

Other Supporters and Helpers:

Thanks to Layne Gering, the former owner of the Clarion Clipper Restaurant who gave our tennis team a free dinner to recognize our PSAC Women's Tennis Championships for four straight years from 1986 to 1989.

Thanks to Paul Weaver, owner of the former Weaver's Jewelry business in Clarion, who gave all the girls on our tennis team a charm and necklace recognizing their achievements as PSAC State Champions for four straight years from 1986 to 1989.

Thanks to those people who have helped me be successful in life as a husband, dad, grandfather, teacher, giver to the community, Clarion Kiwanis member, Women's CUP Head Tennis Coach, Men's CUP Assistant Basketball Coach, Fun with Fundamentals Basketball Director, and Director of Clarion County YMCA "Sportsmanship I" District 9 All-Star Basketball Games. Many of their ideas are found in different aspects of this book. These ideas have come not only from my experiences as a player and coach, interviews with a number of tennis and basketball coaches at all levels, attendance at tennis and basketball practices, individual tennis and basketball workouts, purchase and review of books, and videos of tennis and basketball fundamentals and strategies. I also acquired ideas by studying publications on leadership, teaching, and coaching the great sports of tennis and basketball. I have also attended many tennis and basketball coaching clinics, directed and worked many tennis and basketball camps, looked at many camper evaluations of our camps, and talked to many players and coaches of tennis and basketball over the past four decades.

I want to thank and express my gratitude to all the authors of the books, articles, and videos that I've used over the years and to prepare this book. I also want to thank those who have shared their time, knowledge and talents with me.

In addition, thanks to the many wonderful young women and men whom I have had the personal pleasure of teaching and coaching. I would like to thank my teammates (while participating as a basketball player at Kensington High School and the University of Buffalo, Buffalo, New York), my fellow coaches, faculty, school administrators, dedicated officials, and many community leaders.

TENNIS HISTORY AND ACCOMPLISHMENTS AT CLARION UNIVERSITY

Coaching the Women's Tennis Teams from 1982 – 1989

In 1982 I was appointed Head Women's Varsity Tennis Coach at Clarion University. The year before I was appointed, the 1981 Women's Tennis Team record was 0-9, finished 13 out of 14 schools at the PSAC Women's Tennis Conference Championship, and never had a winning women's tennis season in the school's history.

I had many faculty members and fellow coaches tell me that I would never have a winning women's tennis season at Clarion University because there was very little scholarship aid for women's tennis, and a very little operating budget, and that people just didn't care about women's tennis at Clarion University.

I told the athletic director at Clarion University in 1982 that in 5 years we would win the first ever PSAC women's Tennis Championship for Clarion University. The athletic director told me that I must be smoking some funny stuff or taking drugs because we have never had a winning season in women's tennis in the school's history. I assured him that I had the knowledge, the confidence, the leadership skills, and the recruiting skill level to develop a championship program that would take at least 3 to 5 years of recruiting classes to turn the program around.

The first few years I coached the women's tennis team we struggled, but I wrote and developed our forty-one (41) page team play book which described everything you want your student –athletes to know including: goals for the team, academic required responsibilities including study halls two times a week in the library, individual meetings every two weeks to go over your academic and team responsibilities, practice and game responsibilities, singles and doubles strategies, rules for practice, rules for game travel and conduct, and rewards and punishments stated clearly in advance for proper behavior.

I also wrote a beginning fundamentals tennis book to cover all the fundamentals of tennis and the drills to teach these fundamentals for my tennis teams and tennis classes.

In addition, I also attended many tennis workshops and clinics, visited twenty (20) outstanding Division I, Division II, and Division III tennis college programs, initiated over a one-hundred (100) member Clarion University Women's Tennis Booster Club, improved our fundamentals of tennis, and started to improve our conditioning, our discipline, and our attitude about developing tennis as a successful team sport at Clarion University.

In eight years I developed the best Women's Varsity Tennis Team in Clarion University history and created a dominate tennis dynasty for four years in the Pennsylvania State Athletic Conference Championship.

In my eight seasons as the women's tennis coach, my tennis teams compiled a (72-27) win- loss record, including an astounding (57-1) (98% success rate) dual match record in my last four years. I had four

(4) straight fall season undefeated records. In the National Football League history there is only one team that went undefeated and that was the Miami Dolphins in 1972 (17-0), in which Don Shula was the coach. Any player or coach knows how difficult it is to go undefeated in one year much less four straight years. From 1986 to 1989 Clarion University Women's Tennis Team set the school's all-time number of regular season dual match wins in a row, for all sports, with forty-five (45) consecutive wins. This resulted in a record setting four consecutive PSAC Titles in a row, which was a conference record, twenty four (24) first team All-Pennsylvania State Athletic Conference Tennis Champs, and fourteen (14) Second Team Conference Finalists. In 1989 I also set four (4) PSAC Conference records scoring thirty-one (31) points out of a possible thirty-six (36) points, and was PSAC Champs at #1, #2, #6, Singles and swept the #1, #2, and #3 Doubles Championships, a conference record. Lisa Warren won four straight PSAC #1 Singles titles, a conference record. Lisa Warren was ranked the number 1 singles player in the ITCA East for four years and was ranked nationally as high as 11th in singles and 12th in doubles with Tammy Myers by the ITCA National Division II Tennis Ranking. Lisa Warren was also selected as the 1988 and 1989 "Player of the Year "in the PSAC. In 1989 I also had four singles team members ranked in the Division II ITCA East top ten. Lisa Warren (1), Amanda Bell (4), Tammy Myers (7), and Marianne Martin (9). In 1989, there were two doubles teams ranked in the top four for the Women's Division (II) Tennis East Ranking ITAC: Lisa Warren and Tammy Myers (1), and Lori Berk and Marianne Martin (4). In 1988 and 1989 my tennis team qualified twice for the National NCAA Division (II) Team Championship in which we finished 8th in 1988 and 7th in 1989 in the nation. I was also named "Coach of the Year" in

the PSAC by my peers in both 1988 and 1989. All of these awards and rankings were done with very little scholarships.

I also had a great deal of success with my advising of my tennis teams. Every student-athlete tennis player who played for me for four years during my eight year tenure graduated (100% graduation rate). For eight concurrent semesters from 1986 to 1989, the Clarion Women's Tennis Team academic average was above a 3.0. In 1988, team captain, Jane Bender, was named first team Volvo Tennis Academic All-American and GTE CSIDE (College Sports Information Director of America) Second Team All-America with a 3.93 G. P. A.

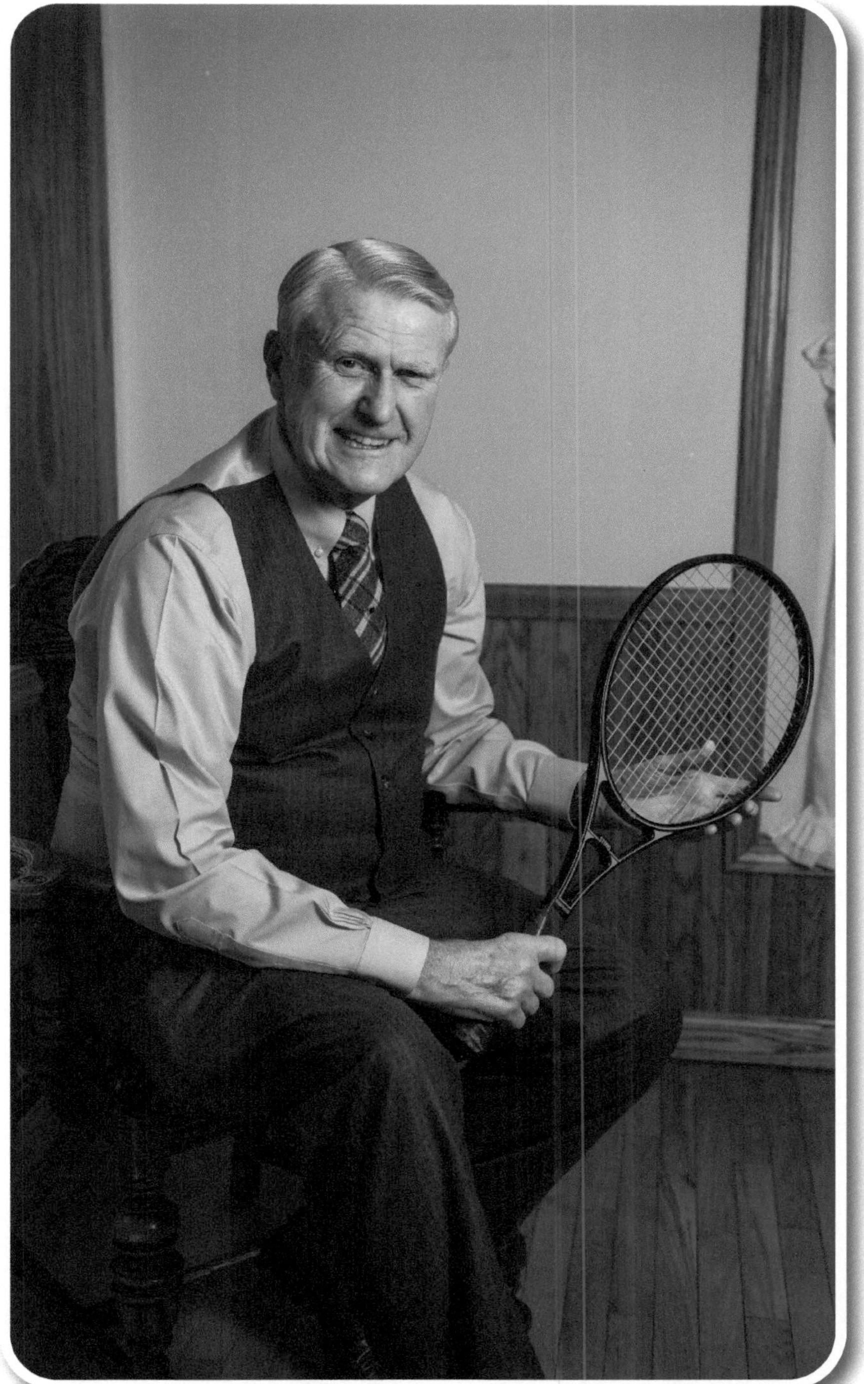

CHAPTER 1

How I recruited student-athletes and built a tennis dynasty at Clarion University with very little scholarships.

RECRUITING – RECRUITING – RECRUITING

I believe that seventy (70%) of your success in coaching on the college level has to be in recruiting quality student-athletes. Without great players you don't win championships.

John Wooden, my mentor, said that if he did not recruit Lew Alcindor, Bill Walton, Sidney Wicks, and many more basketball All-Americans, he would not have won ten (10) Division I Men's NCAA National Championships and have four (4) undefeated seasons in a row and a record of (88-1) at UCLA.

If I did not recruit Lisa Warren Dollard, Susan Fritz, and Tammy Myers, each one with a CUP Hall of Fame Member, and many more number one players for their high school team, we would not have built a tennis dynasty.

What makes my record so awesome and outstanding is that I accomplished these goals with very little scholarships and John Wooden had full scholarships at UCLA.

For any tennis or basketball coach to develop a championship team you need at least eight (8) quality recruits to be competitive and if you want to develop a dynasty you need at least three or four of these quality recruits to be exceptional so that you can dominate your opponents. We had Lisa Warren number (1) singles player the best tennis player in school history who dominated her opponents for four years with a dual match record of (57-1) and Clarion University Hall of fame players Sue Fritz and Tammy Myers to back her up.

In men's basketball you need five(5) quality starters and at least (3) quality subs to be competitive and if you want to dominate your opponents you must have the best men's basketball player in Clarion University history Reggie Wells and NCAA All-Americans Alvin Gibson, and Joe Malis to back him up.

Each individual's greatest chance for growth is in the area of greatest talents and strengths. I believe that one of my top priorities and strengths in my life is that I have proven to be an excellent recruiter. You must know how to choose, you cannot develop to your highest potential in every area of life, a jack of all trades is a master of none, and you need to make choices about where you will grow. Focus on your strengths. The greatest leaders only do a few things exceptionally well. Recruiting is very important to build a sport or life dynasty.

"Independent of others and in concert with others, your main task in life is to do what you can do best and become what you can potentially be" (Erich Fromm).

I have learned a lot about recruiting student-athletes for over (24) years, and I have been the most successful coach and recruiter in the history of Clarion University as the Head Coach of the Women's Tennis Team with very little scholarship aid. Recruiting quality student-athletes is a 24/7 -365 days a year commitment and that doesn't mean you're going to win any games, but you might be competitive. Recruiting quality student-athletes is an art form, time intensive, and requires many hours of communication and persistence.

Over the past 50 + years of teaching and coaching I have used John Wooden's Pyramid of Success to help my students and student-athletes to improve their attitude and help them become better members of our society. I have studied leadership for many years and I believe that my "Triangle to Success" that highlights ten (10) leadership qualities needed to "Build a Sport or Life Dynasty" is a little more simplified and might be easier to understand the reasons for my success and for me, constantly trying to help my students to be significant by helping others.

Below, I will be introducing my 'Triangle to Success" recruiting leadership qualities needed to build a sport or life dynasty: sportsmanship, caring, persistence, skill, hard work, enthusiasm, discipline, teamwork, friendship, and conditioning. One's attitude is key to implementing these leadership qualities.

William James, an American philosopher, psychologist, and educator who lived from 1842 –1910, and considered the "Father of American psychology," offered the first psychology course in the United States and is considered to be a leading thinker and influential philosopher of the late nineteenth century. He believed that one's attitude directly affected the ability to alter one's path. He stated, "The greatest discovery of any generation is that a human being can alter his life by altering his/her attitude". Likewise, I once heard someone state, "A bad attitude is like a flat tire, and you can't go anywhere until you change it."

5

SPORTSMANSHIP

At the top of the "Triangle to Success" I have sportsmanship because I believe it is the most important leadership quality needed to be an effective leader, coach, teacher, and recruiter. To build a sport or life dynasty is to practice sportsmanship in everything that you do.

Sportsmanship is achieved by developing a positive attitude, knowing and playing by the rules, having fun, playing your best, and most important, being honest and truthful. A person must be sincere and honest in every phase of his life. He/she might lack something in knowledge and technique and still get along, but his or her fate is failure if he/she is lacking in honesty or sincerity. Recruits will not change, work hard, or believe in you if they do not trust your honesty and sincerity.

Abraham Lincoln said, "All other successes would follow in the footsteps of honesty and integrity, make honesty your goal, are you ambitiously pursuing integrity? "

I have researched sportsmanship for over fifty (50) years, and I believe it is the most important leadership quality you need to build a sport or life dynasty. Below are some of the definitions of what I think "sportsmanship" means, for sportsmanship is highly useful to a coach or human being to be a great role model.

Sportsmanship requires self-control and mental toughness. You must keep your emotions under control and must be able to think clearly at all times. You must be fair, consistent, and keep your poise at all times. You must keep your emotions under control. There is a delicate adjustment between mind and body. You must have good judgement and common sense. You must be responsible for your actions, or inactions toward others, including your own team members, your coaches, your administrators, your opponents, and your officials, friends, and family.

Sportsmanship requires one to practice good manners. As my mother often said to me, "There is no substitute for good manners." She stressed that courtesy means being respectful and considerate of others, having excellent manners of social conduct, being friendly and humble if you win, and learning from your mistakes if you lose. Sportsmanship is not blaming others or making excuses for your mistakes and weaknesses. It is being flexible enough to improve or change tactics when necessary.

Sportsmanship is treating the people that you play with and against as you'd like to be treated yourself. Give your best and shake hands with your opponents before and after a game or match. Thank the other team or individual for giving you a challenge and being competitive. Congratulate your opponents.

Sportsmanship is demonstrating positive character traits which are essential components of leadership. But what is character?

Character is defined by the way a person normally responds to desires, fears, challenges, opportunities, habits, failures, and successes. It is displaying one's disposition, values, and actions when no one is looking.

Character is the most essential component of excellent leadership. Character is perseverance after the initial excitement has worn off. It is crashing through the quitting point.

Character, regardless of your job or profession, should not be bought out by any political pressure, code of loyalty, code of silence, individual, special interest group, or policy. You must have the courage to stand-up and speak-up and do the right thing for everyone involved. If you remain silent, you are not practicing good sportsmanship.

Character is defined by qualities of fairness, courtesy, and trust.

Fairness is when one plays by the rules that are unbiased, equitable, just, honest and impartial. One treats all sides with respect, justly, and equitably. Ultimately, the "Golden Rule" is about fairness and decency and treating people right.

Courtesy means being respectful and considerate of others and having excellent manners of social conduct. There is no substitute for good manners.

Sportsmanship involves qualities of trust. As Gandhi once stated, "One of the most essential qualities of the human spirit is to trust one another and to build trust with others." Wilfred Peterson described an effective leader as one who has faith in people and believes in his followers, trusts them, and thus draws out the best in them. David L. Minio in *The Importance of Trust in Leadership* states, "Trust is the glue that binds leaders and followers together. Trust implies reliability, predictability, and common concern for others. Trust is an emotional strength that begins with a feeling of self-worth and purpose that we're called to extend outward to others. The warm, solid gut feeling you get from counting on yourself and trusting and being trusted by others. This is one of the great enablers of life with it, we have the inner room to grow, to become emotionally fit, and to exercise and expand our capacity to build bridges from one issue to another, one idea to another, and one person to another."

Abraham Lincoln's words are worth remembering. He said, "It is better to trust and occasionally be disappointed than to mistrust and be miserable all the time."

Recruit good people, teach them, train them, and then have courage enough to trust them to do what they're supposed to do. When others understand us and know who we are, they will then know what matters to us. Robert K. Cooper - 2010 - Body, Mind & Spirit states, "We must feel that they care about us, and that they will weigh our true needs, interests, and concerns when they make decisions."

Sportsmanship is one of the most important components of leadership. You must have a good work ethic and a ceaseless desire to improve. You must constantly be looking for ways to be innovative and improve, willing to sacrifice as an individual for the good of the group, compete hard, be humble in both victory and defeat, and exhibit good sportsmanship and integrity at all times. The mark of a true leader and someone who practices excellent sportsmanship is that one admits that he/she has made a mistake and apologizes. Everyone makes mistakes, and the greatest leaders, coaches, and people who build dynasties have the honesty, compassion, kindness, and courage to admit that they have made a mistake, apologizes, and try to make it right for everyone involved.

Knute Rockne, Notre Dame Football coach said," One man practicing sportsmanship is better than a hundred teaching it."

CARING

The second most important leadership quality you need for the "Triangle to Success" is you must care about every individual. This is one of the reasons why I have caring as one of the foundations of my "Triangle to Success". The truly great leaders, coaches, and recruiters not only care and respect each individual, but also show a strong sense of compassion, empathy and fairness to each individual. An effective leader, coach, and recruiter recognize the importance of building relationships. I would not recruit a basketball player or tennis player if we did not have a major that they were interested in. I believe honesty and a caring attitude are the main reasons why I had success in recruiting great student-athletes at the University of Buffalo and Clarion University.

I would make a pledge to all my recruits and parents that I would do all in my power to make sure that their daughter or son will graduate

IN FOUR YEARS. I cared about each tennis player or basketball player as if they were my daughter or son and, as Head Tennis Coach at CUP, we had 100% graduation rate for all women tennis players who played four years for me.

John Wooden believed that "a caring attitude was an essential ingredient to success." It was his opinion that, "people do not care how much you know until they know how much you care". I applied this philosophy to how I treated my tennis teams, basketball teams, players, students, fellow coaches, friends, and family,

To teach or coach is to touch a life. A caring teacher and/or coach touches the lives of many. I use each evaluation to tell me how well I help my students and players to learn.

PERSISTENCE

The third most important leadership quality you need to build a sport or life dynasty is persistence. This is why I have persistence as one of the corner-foundations of my "Triangle to Success". Genius is 1% inspiration and 99 % perspiration, which means that persistence is probably one of the most critical leadership qualities you need for success. Persistence is a commitment to a goal. With the leadership quality of persistence, you must believe in yourself, you must have confidence, and you must have consistent stick-to-itiveness. Bull-dog mentality, self-control, and mental toughness are crucial for recruiting quality student - athletes. In successful recruiting, the game begins for me when the outstanding recruit says "no."

Lou Holtz, Head Football Coach at Notre Dame University who won a Division I National Championship stated, "In my mind, persistence is the most critical to success and happiness. Nothing takes the place of persistence. Talent won't. Nothing is more common than unsuccessful men or women with talent. Genius won't do it. Unrewarding genius is almost a proverb. Education will not. The world is full of educated derelicts. Persistence alone is omnipotent."

NBA Basketball All-Star for the New York Knicks (Bill Bradley) "Ambition is the path to success; persistence is the vehicle you arrive in."

Professional golfer and "King" of Golf Arnold Palmer) said, "Persistence is a commitment to a goal. The most rewarding things you do in life are often the ones that look like they cannot be done." If I would have listened to our athletic director, coaches, faculty at CUP and quit, we would never have built the Women's Tennis Dynasty at Clarion University for four (4) years in the PSAC Conference.

Below, I have listed personal examples of my persistence leading to my success.

1. As mentioned earlier, my brother Charles beat me one hundred (100) straight games in a row of one-on-one basketball games. I finally beat him and never lost a one-on-one game to him thereafter. This experience was very humbling to me and helped me develop my sportsmanship and persistence. My persistence in trying to beat my older brother and his friends gave me valuable experience to raise my level of basketball competition and play. That experience gave me the confidence to dominate my own age level of competition and make First Team Basketball High School All-Western New York and First Team Basketball All-City Buffalo, New York my senior year. Twice I was voted MVP by my teammates as a walk-on for the University of Buffalo Men's Basketball Team. I was also voted as NCAA Division II First Team All-Tournament Quarter Finalist Basketball Team. In addition, I

was selected to play in the East-West College All-Star Basketball Game in Erie, PA my senior year, in which our team set a school record of 19-3, a 86 % winning percentage.

2. During my junior year at Kensington High School in Buffalo, New York, my homeroom and English teacher told me I would never graduate from college because I did not have the academic skills to be a success in college. My father only went to the sixth grade because at age 12, his father died of a heart attack and he had to drop out of school and become the bread winner for his mother and 5 brothers and sisters. My mother only went to eighth grade, so chances of me finishing college were slim and none. I was a walk-on for the Men's Basketball Team my first semester at the University of Buffalo S.U.N.Y. I paid my own tuition, fees, and books myself because my mother and father had no money to send me to college. During the second semester of my freshmen year, I met with Dr. Leonard Serfustini, my Head Men's Basketball Coach, and the Head Freshmen Basketball Coach, Ed Muto, at the University of Buffalo. They informed me that my mother and father earned too much money and that I could not receive a full scholarship if I lived at home. I told my teammates on the Men's Freshmen Basketball Team that I was going to have to drop out of school because I did not have enough money to pay for my tuition, fees, and books my second semester. Our freshmen team played Niagara University the next day and I scored 25 points, 12 rebounds and hit the winning shot to beat Niagara University for the freshmen team. The next day I was called into Coach Serfustini's and Coach Muto's office and I received a full scholar-

ship which paid for my tuition, fees, and books for three and a half years. They also gave me a job as student-assistant athletic trainer for the UB football team for three and a half years, which helped pay me back the cost of my first semester expenses. I took 18 hours of credit each semester, never failed a class or had to go to summer school and graduated in four years with a B. ED. In Health and Physical Education (1965). I went on to earn my Masters in Health and Physical Education at UB in (1968), and I have over 100 hours of graduate courses completed in Leadership and Administration.

3. Many faculty, administrators, family, and friends told me I would never get my Full- Professor Ranking at Clarion University without my doctorate. After applying thirty-three (33) times for full Professor at Clarion University, I was granted a Full Professorship in 2013. I was very persistent until I accomplished my goal.

4. On March 6, 1992, I initiated the movement to start a YMCA in Clarion County by calling a meeting at the Clarion County Court House. Many people told me others tried to have a YMCA in Clarion County but that will never happen and we will fail too. For the past twenty-eight (28) years I have been very persistent and have worked extremely hard raising large amounts of money with others - approximately $745,000 - for the Clarion County YMCA so that they could stay in existence. In the summer of 2017, we had a ground breaking for a new twelve (12) million dollar YMCA built at the 18th fairway at the Clarion Oakes Golf Course.

5. Lisa Warren Dollard, the best player ever to play tennis at Clarion University, had many scholarship offers out of high school, and she told me at least five (5) times that she wanted to go play tennis with her older sister who was the captain of the University of Louisville Women's Tennis Team, but I continued to recruit Lisa until she called me and said she wanted to come to Clarion University and major in Elementary Education. Lisa said, "I had other offers, but Coach Baschnagel was extremely passionate for his love of Clarion and their athletics. This came through very clearly in our conversations, and I decided to make Clarion my collegiate home. On the court, Coach Baschnagel was an enthusiastic trainer and instructor. His philosophy is deeply rooted in self-improvement, hard work, and integrity. He was a mentor and role model for our entire team. Off the court, Coach Baschnagel constantly monitored our studies to guarantee that we all graduated with honors."

6. Susan Fritz shared her story; "At my induction to the Clarion University Sports Hall of Fame in 2019, I shared the story of how I ended up at Clarion. I was offered a scholarship at Edinboro University and had planned on going there, as my 2 older siblings were already attending Edinboro. I felt that was my fate. After visiting Clarion University with my parents and hearing his approach to coaching and his philosophy on what a student-athlete should be, my parents knew that this was where I wanted to go and needed to be. There was no scholarship money, but my parents knew that Coach Baschnagel would develop me as an athlete, a student, and, more importantly a

better person who would be prepared to be a positive role model and ready to face the world outside of Clarion."

7. Tamara Myers shared her recruiting story. "While being recruited by Coach Baschnagel, I was struck by his passion, dedication and commitment to the university and the tennis program. This drive and persistence is what ultimately moved me to become a student-athlete at Clarion from the fall of 1987 to the spring of 1991. Those same characteristics that intrigued me as a recruit were magnified in his coaching style. He taught us many valuable lessons that helped not only on and off the court, but also instilled values that stayed with us throughout our lives. We learned about hard work, dedication, commitment, courage, perseverance, self-control, unity and what it takes to win as a team. From the beginning "Coach B" had our best interests at heart, pushing us to be our best in every aspect of our lives. He stressed the importance of a quality education, leading our team to average a 3.0 GPA or above, to have integrity and to strive for excellence both on and off the court.

8. Above all Coach Baschnagel is a man of integrity who was a great role model that led by example, and his leadership didn't stop at just being an awesome coach. As players, we witnessed his dedication, loyalty and love for his family as well as great service to his community around him. That influence has positively impacted our lives and has contributed to many of our successes still" (Tamara Myers –CUP Alumni, 91, and CUP Athletic Sports Hall of Fame)

If I was not persistent in recruiting Lisa, Susan, Tammy, and many other outstanding women varsity tennis players, we would not have built the women's tennis dynasty. Persistence is a commitment to a goal with determination and you never give up.

"Persistence and determination alone are omnipotent"
(Calvin Coolidge).

ENTHUSIASM

The next recruiting key to the "Triangle to Success" an building a tennis dynasty at Clarion University was that I was the most <u>"Enthusiastic, "Passionate", and "Dedicated</u> –person about the Women's Tennis Team, and I recruited student-athletes first and cared about my players as if I had twelve (12) daughters. I tried to instill in my players, family first, academics second, and tennis third.

Enthusiasm means lively, absorbing interest, and excited involvement. It is also defined as intense and eager enjoyment. One of the team's greatest resources is the enthusiasm, passion, and dedication of its tennis players. Enthusiasm tends to rub off on the players with whom the coaching staff comes in contact and the enthusiastic players tend to inspire and stimulate others. As the Coach, your heart must be in your work if you are to progress, as it will make you eager to improve and learn. (John Wooden) used to say "The sky's the limit when your heart is in it".

"Success is the ability to go from failure to failure without you losing your enthusiasm" (Winston Churchill)

Passion is a practical necessity. It is the driving force of your heart and soul. It engages your excitement for activities that matter most to you and leads to inner happiness. In recruiting student-athletes you must have passion and enthusiasm because you will have many disappointments in recruiting but you must not lose your enthusiasm and dedication to accomplish all your goals. I believe, you can't light the fire of passion and dedication in someone else if it doesn't burn in you to begin with. I had a real burning desire and passion to promote the women's tennis program at Clarion University and I was not going to stop until we built a tennis dynasty "We may affirm that nothing great in the world has been accomplished without passion" (Hegel) "We are shaped and guided by what we love to do" (Goethe).

Dedication is the devotion to a certain way, in this case the lifestyle of a champion, in order to make the most out of oneself, to discover just how darn good you can be. Dedication is a deeper stronger, more passionate level of commitment. Being dedicated is that spiritual space that embraces failures, fatigue, setbacks, mistakes, frustrations, suffering and sacrifices on the journey of being "The best that you can be". It requires fundamental faith, trust, and confidence in the process, as you display patience and perseverance that all the hard work will pay off for you to become a champion. Being dedicated means a certain willingness to do all that is required to grow and improve, even if you sometimes don't feel like doing it. Commitment is the major ingredient that separates those who break on through to the other side and experience personal greatness from those who don't. True commitment is devotion to a cause, ideal or goal. Dedication is the willingness to do all that is necessary to grow and improve as an athlete and person to build a sport or life dynasty. Any leader, teacher, or coach who is reading this, you know you must have

17

enthusiasm, passion, and dedication, and your heart must be into coaching and reaching your goals because you are going to have many ups and downs. If you are not passionate about reaching your goals, you might take the easy way out and quit.

Amid all the talk about enthusiasm, passion, and dedication you want to make sure that your players and recruits must have fun at your practices and tennis matches because if the practices and games are not fun your players will not perform for you and they will possibly quit. It is very important that your players and potential recruits look forward to practice and the games and that you do not become way too serious. I believe that my practices would not be more than two hours long and that each practice would have a detailed written practice outline which I worked preparing every day. I believe you must do the little fundamental things right. Planning and preparation are essential components of your practices. Practice should be organized, disciplined, and at the same time it must be fun. Sportsmanship is the most important thing you must teach at your practices and tennis matches and that each recruit or player must practice sportsmanship first and be considerate of others.

HARD WORK

The next recruiting key to the "Triangle to Success" and building a sport or life dynasty is hard work. No one was going to outwork me. There is no substitute for hard work and meticulous planning.

Industriousness refers to hard working, diligent, and energetic. Many of us have heard the phrase, "There is no substitute for hard work." Worthwhile results come from hard work and careful planning. My dad told me many times, "The harder you work, the luckier you get." If you want to take your skills to the next level, there is only one option, and that is hard work. A good work ethic is the foundation on which you build the goals you equate with success.

One might even say that a continuous good effort is the definition of success because it teaches us so much about ourselves and how we want to live. If you hope to experience overall success you must keep improving and striving to reach your potential. You will never have success unless you stretch yourself. If you're always in your comfort zone, you're not achieving your full potential. Success is a matter of personal accountability. Only you know whether you're capable of stretching yourself even more and becoming better at what you do. If you can say that you know you can do better, yet choose to stay in your comfort zone, then you cannot claim to be having success, even though you may appear to be successful to some people. Therefore, you should continue to work hard every day to improve and make yourself a better person, as there is no substitute for hard work. Work matters, but curiosity matters more. Nobody works harder than a curious person who wants to make adaptive change for the good of mankind. All worthwhile accomplishments require sacrifice and hard work.

I believe this poem by Henry Wadsworth Longfellow explains how important "Hard Work" is:

> The heights by great men reached and kept
> We're not attained by sudden flight,
> But they, while their companions slept,
> We're toiling upward in the night.

This poem by Longfellow is very important for you to be the best hard working person in your organization and lead by example and be the first person at work each day.

CBS-60 Minutes had a documentary on Head Coach Bill Belichick of the New England Patriots who won (6) "Super Bowls" and he is the first one at work each day at (5:30 A.M.)

Many times I would have trouble sleeping and I would wake up very early and work at recruiting and coaching projects in the middle of the night because the house would be very quiet and make it very easy to concentrate. My wife and I had four children and we were very busy raising our four children and accomplishing our teaching and coaching responsibilities.

As a leader, coach, recruiter, and steward for your community you must have a good attitude and practice my "Triangle to Success" leadership qualities of sportsmanship, caring, persistence, enthusiasm, and hard work, so you can build your own sport or life dynasty.

RESEARCH ON RECRUITING

As Assistant Men's Basketball Coach and Head Women's Tennis Coach, one of my major responsibilities was recruiting excellent student-athletes. Those in academia may not generally understand or appreciate how important recruiting is in sports or life. It is the "heart" of a program and excellence is absolutely necessary if the sport is to succeed or excel. Recruiting, both an art and a skill, is time intensive and requires great patience and perseverance. Much of my success in basketball and tennis recruiting was due to my very successful recruiting procedures and skills which are listed below.

RECRUITING PROCEDURES FOR STUDENT ATHLETES

Below are my very successful recruiting procedures and skills that I used at Clarion University of PA

1. The first procedure in recruiting a student athlete was to mail a recruiting form letter, questionnaire, athletic schedule, business card, and return postage paid envelope to approximately 500 high school junior prospects from Pennsylvania, Ohio, New York, New Jersey, and West Virginia. Today, these can be sent by email.

2. Then send a follow-up letter requesting a high school transcript to every prospect who returned his/her questionnaire.

3. Send each prospect that was interested a university application, catalog, and admission's handbook.

4. See the prospect play at least twice at a high school practice, match, or game.

5. Since Clarion University is located two hours from any major city with a large population, I spent many hours visiting coaches, guidance counselors, and prospects at their high schools and their homes. At this personal visit, I would present a picture book and slide show presentation which I developed with our Communication Department to the recruit and his/her parents. I would also give each recruit a media guide to help explain the success of our program.

6. I would send a follow-up letter and telephone call every time I saw the prospect play or visited his/her school or home.

7. Throughout the entire recruiting process, a call was made to the prospect every other week and we would send press clippings about our team (Eagle Talk Newsletter) every week or on holiday cards.

8. We scheduled personal visits by the prospect and his/her parents to the University. This step was crucial in the recruiting process. It included the following:

A. I made up a detailed itinerary for the entire visit where every minute was accounted for.

B. I would coordinate meetings with admissions, financial aid, and a meeting with faculty member in his/her major, a student tutorial, and a dormitory supervisor.

C. I also arranged meals and visits with our student-athletes to show the recruits the campus and community to conclude his/her campus visit.

D. I met in my office with the recruit and parents and made a detailed presentation of all of the advantages of attending Clarion University.

E. I explained the goals of our program and the commitment to excellence that is needed to be successful in the classroom and on the court.

F. I presented each prospect with a season summary that I compiled throughout the entire year of our team accomplishments.

G. I usually gave the recruit 2 weeks to make a final decision if he/she was going to attend Clarion University in the fall.

H. I would send each prospect a check list on why they should choose Clarion University.

This checklist would outline the many positive aspects for attending Clarion University and was a very valuable recruiting instrument. See below.

CLARION UNIVERSITY "GOLDEN EAGLE"
CHECKLIST FOR CHOOSING A SCHOOL

This list represents a number of suggestions to help you decide which college or university, among those you are considering, that would be the best fit for you. The major areas of concern are your academic life, your athletic career, and your social life._

The purpose of this checklist is very simple. Take the schools that you are thinking of attending and compare them in the categories listed. The colleges and universities that best measure up to the list are probably going to be your best choices.

Athletes, too often, postpone the process of deciding which schools would be best for them until the last minute. As a result, sometimes hasty decisions are made that prove to be unsatisfactory later. This will assist you in the process of eliminating schools that do not measure up. It will help you narrow your choices to three or four universities that compare favorably in the areas considered. Once you are down to a few choices it may be necessary to visit the campus and surrounding community before reaching the important final decision. Thus, you can understand the need to begin this process early. A student-athlete concerned with the future will have narrowed down his/her choices to three or four schools by the end of his/her senior fall season at the latest. Then he/she will be ready to make some campus visits before making a definite final decision.

I offer this checklist so that you may begin the elimination process early, leaving adequate time upon which you can base a wise and well-informed decision.

CHECKLIST (REFERENCE TO 1982-1989)
CLARION UNIVERSITY

1. Range of Undergraduate Academic Offerings
    - Clarion University offers course work leading to a Bachelor's Degree in 66 fields and conducts organized research in several specialized fields.

2. Range of Graduate Academic Offerings
    - Clarion University offers course work leading toward the Master's Degree in 12 fields of study.

3. Academic Standing
    - Clarion University is fully accredited by the Middle States Association of Colleges and Schools, accredited by the National Council for Accreditation of Teacher Education and approved by the American Chemical Society.

4. Outstanding Fields of Study where the University is strong.
    - School of Education and Human Service
    - School of Communication
    - School of Business Administration
    - School of Arts and Sciences
    - School of Library Science

5. Size of University
    - Today Clarion University is a multi-purpose institution with an enrollment of approximately 5,000 students.

6. Class Size

- Most classes on campus average about eighteen (18) students per professor.

7. Tutoring Services available through the university.
   - Yes – available to all students. Arrangements made through the coaches and athletic department.

8. Campus Setting
   - The main campus of the university contains ninety-nine acres and thirty-eight buildings, the majority of which were constructed within the past twenty years.
   - Beyond the main campus, situated at the west end of the town of Clarion, is a 27 acre athletic complex with football, baseball, and practice fields for intramurals and recreation. The Memorial Stadium, seats 5000 spectators. The University is within the borough of Clarion, some two miles north of interstate 80 at exits 9 and 10 and is approximately two hours driving time from the urban centers of Pittsburgh and Erie. High on the Allegheny Plateau overlooking the Clarion River, the rural setting is among the most beautiful in the East.

9. Residential Life
   - Clarion's residential life is unique in many different ways. The dorms are gradually becoming more than just a place to eat and sleep; they are changing to a Center of Social Interaction for its residents and neighboring halls. Major halls sponsor activities such as lecture series, dances, coffee house, and live entertainment.

10. Weather

- When you arrive in Clarion you will probably be greeted by a warm, Indian summer. Before too long Indian summer gives way to a crisp and colorful fall. The first snow usually appears in late November. The changing seasons in Clarion are at their best, offering various activities for each type of weather conditions. Autumn is ideal for walks through campus and downtown Clarion. The winter scenery is often breathtaking when the snow reflects the bright sunshine. Spring and summer are probably the most enjoyable times bringing the warm days. Many classes are moved outdoors to enjoy these days.

11. Recreational Sports Opportunities

- The rolling wooded countryside, interspersed with small farms, affords some of the most enjoyable outdoor activities to be found anywhere in Northwestern Pennsylvania. Endless outdoor sporting opportunities feature hunting, fishing, golf, tennis, and the Clarion River and Cook Forest provides an excellent setting for summer boating, swimming, and aquatic sports.

12. Student Affairs

- Clarion University is concerned not only with the academic development of young men and women, but also with their development as mature, self-confident, socially competent adults. To assist this development, various student personnel services are provided. These services enable those enrolled in the university to perform more adequately as students and to derive benefits from the academic, cultural, social, and recreational opportunities offered by the campus environment. In addition, every administrative and teaching member of the faculty is charged with the responsibility of assisting students to select and achieve goals consistent with the ideals of a university community.

13. Campus Life
   • Campus life at Clarion is relaxed and what you make it to be. Dress includes T-shirts, shorts, and sandals for fall and spring, while dungarees and sweaters are appropriate for winter. Occasionally dress clothes are needed for parties such as those sponsored by fraternities or sororities during the holidays or spring formals.

14. Type of Surrounding Community
   • Clarion is a small college town of approximately 6,000 people. The university extends into the life of the town and, likewise, students participate in community activities such as community theatre, community choir, and Clarion's own Autumn Leaf Festival which is held each October. Clarion houses many churches of various faiths and the Clarion Osteopathic Community Hospital. Merchants in town and at the Clarion Mall always welcome Clarion University students.

15. Career Placement Services
   • The Office of Career Planning and Placement provides services related to Career information and placement to

all students and alumni who desire them. Seminars are conducted for juniors and seniors concerning necessary job entry skills. Graduate School information is also maintained along with various test applications for entry into Graduate School.

16. Head Coach – (example) For any sport, the recruits and parents want to know the background and success of the head coach and this write-up could also be used in your media guide from your sports information director.

- Clarion University's rise to PSAC and national prominence can be credited to Head Coach Norb Baschnagel who begins his 8th season as the Golden Eagles Mentor.

- In 1988-89 Norb led his team to its third straight PSAC Championship, plus its second straight NCAA Division II Playoff berth. Baschnagel, himself, received the spoils of the strong team effort by being named the PSAC "Coach of the Year". The team posted an impressive 16-1 dual meet record last season with the only downfall coming at the hand of Division I power Penn State. In the previous two years the Eagles had posted perfect slates of 15-0 and 13-0 in 1986-87 for a (44-1) dual meet record entering 1989. Never having a winning season prior to his arrival, Baschnagel has taken Women's Tennis at Clarion to new heights in each of his first seven seasons. Coach "B" stresses the "Clarion Tennis Way" which reflects his overall philosophy in developing a delicate balance between team and individual play.

- A native of Buffalo, New York, Norb graduated from Kensington High School in 1961. An outstanding basketball player in High School, he concentrated his efforts in basketball when he attended the University of Buffalo. There, he earned M.V.P. post season honors after his freshmen and senior campaigns. He was selected to play in two post season NCAA College Division Tournaments and played in the East- West College All-Star game in Erie, PA in 1965.

- Baschnagel was a member of the SUNY at Buffalo faculty from 1967 to 1974. Coach Baschnagel taught tennis for several years there and coached it for one year as the Head Coach of the Men's Tennis team and registered a 12-4 record and was ranked 5th in the East in Division II. Norb also earned his Bachelor's Degree in 1965 and also received his Master's Degree in Health and Physical Education in 1968, also at SUNY at Buffalo.

- Norb has been employed at Clarion University since 1974 in the Health and Physical Education Department. Before serving as women's tennis coach Baschnagel was Assistant Men's Basketball Coach at Clarion for eight seasons. During that time period the Golden Eagles averaged 20 wins per year. The 1976-77 campaign saw Clarion win 27-games (27-3), the most wins in a single season.

- A student of the game, Baschnagel's tennis background is also quite extensive, thus his nomination as an Eastern NCAA Regional Chairperson for the 1989 season. He has attended the Dennis Vandemere School of Tennis while also visiting a number of the top tennis programs on the West Coast, plus various other tennis workshops, clinics, and camps throughout his career. He has also organized the first successful tennis camp at Clarion University during the summer, plus has an open tennis tournament during (8) Autumn Leaf Festivals week each fall.

- As former Department Chairman and Full Professor at Clarion in the Health and Physical Education Department, Baschnagel has had articles published in Research Quarterly, Scholastic Coach and has written (3) books on *How to Direct Successful Fun with Fundamental Basketball Camps*. Beginning his 16th year at Clarion, Norb resides in Clarion with his wife, Beverly and their four children, daughters Heidi and Grace, and sons Charles and Peter.

OUTSTANDING STUDENT-ATHLETES WHO I RECRUITED:
When I recruited these student-athletes I knew within fifteen (15) minutes after watching them play or practice that these players were Division I players that could help our tennis and basketball teams possibly win a National Championship in Division II. My philosophy in recruiting student-athletes for Clarion University was that you must reach and stretch yourself and get out of your comfort zone for the five-star players and recruit players who want to go to Division I and sell them on the fact that if they come to Clarion University that the following Division I student-athletes could possibly win a National Title in Tennis and Basketball at the Division II level.

The success of building a dynasty starts with recruiting.

I have successfully recruited the following outstanding student-athletes to represent Clarion University's Men's Basketball Teams and Women's Tennis Teams. Listed below are some of my successfully recruited student-athletes.

- Clarion University Sports Hall of Fame inducted members who I recruited:

  + 2019   Susan Fritz   Tennis
  + 2011   Tammy Myers   Tennis
  + 2007   Chris Roosevelt   Basketball
  + 2006   Carl Grinage   Basketball
  + 2003   Daniel Chojnacki   Basketball
  + 2001   Joseph Malis   Basketball
  + 2000   Lisa M. Warren   Tennis
  + 1999   Michael C. Sisinni   Basketball
  + 1997   Alvin E. Gibson   Basketball
  + 1996   Terry E. Roseto   Basketball
  + 1995   John V. Calipari   Basketball
  + 1990   Reginald A. Wells   Basketball

Tammy Meyers stated in a letter of recommendation for me into the CUP Sports Hall of Fame, "Twelve student-athletes who were coached and recruited by Coach Baschnagel have subsequently been elected into the Clarion University Sports Athletic Hall of Fame for their outstanding achievements. This is a testament to his exemplary coaching and recruiting skills and shows he did what he was hired to do; in fact he went above and beyond. Clearly, it is his turn to be selected with this prestigious honor."

- Tamara Myers tennis captain and CUP Hall of Fame 91 (August 20, 2019)

OTHER RECRUITING SUCCESSES
ACCOMPLISHED AT CLARION UNIVERSITY

- Two (2) Presidential Scholarship Recipients
  - Mike Sisinni , Men's Basketball CUP Hall of Fame -1999
  - Jeffrey Szumigale, Men's Basketball, former member of the Board of Trustees of Clarion University

CLARION UNIVERSITY MEN'S
BASKETBALL AWARDS 1978 TO 1982

Reggie Wells - 1978

H M: NAIA Honorable All-American

1st Team: District 18 and ECAC

Reggie Wells – 1979

NAIA All-American

1st Team: PSAC

1st Team: ECAC and District 18

1st Team: Press and Post-Gazette_

1979 PSAC All – Conference

1st Team: Reggie Wells

2nd Team: Mike Sisinni

H. M.:   Dan Chojnacki, Jeff Ebner

1979 District 18 Team

1st Team: Reggie Wells

2nd Team: Mike Sisinni

1980 PSAC All-Conference

1st Team: Alvin Gibson

2nd Team: Terry Johnson, Dan Chojnacki

1981 – Alvin Gibson

3rd Team: NCAA Div. II All-American

2nd Team: NAIA All-American

1st Team: ECAC and District 18

1st Team: Pittsburgh. Press and Post – Gazette

Pittsburgh Press and Post – Gazette – Small College "Player of the Year"

1982 – Joseph Malis

2nd Team: NCAA Div. II All-American (6th in overall voting)

1st Team: ECAC and District 18

1st Team: Pittsburgh. Press and Post – Gazette

Pittsburgh Press and Post – Gazette "Small College Player of the Year"

NCAA Division II Second Team All- American Players

1979 – Reggie Wells

1981 – Alvin Gibson

1982 – Joe Malis

CLARION UNIVERSITY WOMEN'S TENNIS PSAC STATE CHAMPS (24)
1986

Lisa Warren – Number 1 Singles

Susan Fritz – Number 2 Singles

Amanda Bell – Number 3 Singles

Lynne Fye – Number 4 Singles

Lynne Fye and Susan Fritz – Number 2 Doubles

1987

Lisa Warren – Number 1 Singles

Tammy Myers – Number 4 Singles

Lisa Warren and Susan Fritz – Number 1 Doubles

1988

Lisa Warren – Number 1 Singles

Jane Bender – Number 5 Singles

Rosie Kramarski – Number 6 Singles

Amanda Bell and Lori Kohn – Number 3 Doubles

1989

Lisa Warren – Number 1 Singles

Amanda Bell – Number 2 Singles

Lori Berk - Number 6 Singles

Lisa Warren and Tammy Myers – Number 1 Doubles

Lori Berk and Marianne Martin – Number 2 Doubles

Amanda Bell and Lori Kohn – Number 3 Doubles

CLARION UNIVERSITY WOMEN'S
TENNIS STATE FINALIST (14)
1986

Jane Bender – Number 5 Singles

1987

Susan Fritz – Number 2 Singles

Amanda Bell – Number 3 Singles

Carolyn Vallecorsa – Number 5 Singles

Jane Bender – Number 6 Singles

Tammy Myers and Lori Kohn – Number 2 Doubles

Amanda Bell and Debra McAdams – Number 3 doubles

1988

Tammy Myers – Number 2 Singles

Amanda Bell – Number 3 Singles

Lisa Warren and Tammy Myers – Number 1 Doubles

1989

Lori Kohn – Number 5 Singles

1988-89 Two (2) Tennis Player of the Year Awards in the PSAC

Lisa Warren twice

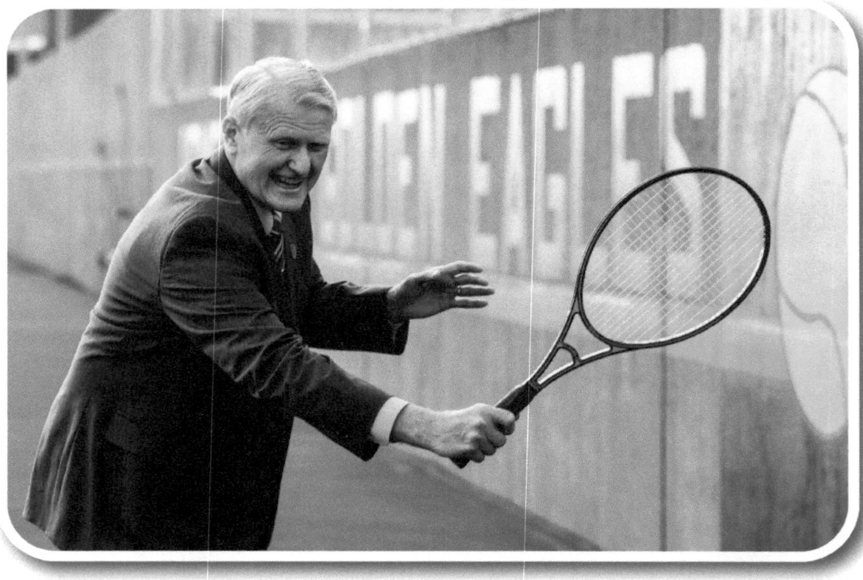
EAGLES

CHAPTER 2

*I believe that 25% of your success in building
a sport or life dynasty is in coaching:*

COACHING – COACHING – COACHING

My philosophy of Coaching Women's Tennis and War Cry at Clarion University was Serve – Attack – Volley. I believe that when a dual-match was against a tough opponent that the winner of the match would be decided by the three (3) doubles dual-match points.

If you stay back and don't Serve-Attack –Volley with your partner your chances of winning the match are slim and none. You and your partner must attack aggressively at all times. I wanted our opponents to know that when they played Clarion University at our home court, that we would be the aggressor and that we would constantly be attacking our opponents and dominating the action.

I wanted my teams to constantly put pressure on our opponents until they would crack. To play this aggressive style of tennis I believe our teams were the best conditioned teams in the country both physically and mentally. To back –up this statement our Women's Tennis Team was undefeated at home the last four years that I coached tennis (1986-1989).

DISCIPLINE

The first leadership quality in my "Triangle to Success" you need to build a sport or life dynasty in coaching is you must have discipline, which means the practice of training people to obey rules of a code of behavior and using punishment to correct disobedience because you can't teach or coach any student-athlete without discipline. This is possible only when you have the ability to control yourself. If you don't have the discipline to control yourself, how do you expect to exercise control of your team?

WHY IS IT IMPORTANT TO BE DISCIPLINED?

The most successful people in life exert discipline on a daily basis, for discipline is vital to every living being to help avoid chaos. Discipline brings stability and structure into a person's life and it teaches a person to be responsible and respectful. It is an important requirement for studying and learning, for developing any skill, and for success in self-improvement, spiritual growth, and meditation. Discipline is essential to your character to help train a person's mind, build character, and increase a sense of self control and obedience. External discipline according to societal norms is following the law. We need not only to possess great character qualities; we also need the ability to manage them. Discipline is a way of life where one tries to be on time and live in a systematic way. Discipline is not limited to money, riches, or by poverty, but it is a personal orientation toward life. Many successful people attribute their success to discipline. Consistency at high levels,

I believe, is the mark of great leadership. Self-control contributes to consistency in all areas that matter.

To build a sport or life dynasty you need a playbook and a book of fundamentals in a particular sport. I had a Tennis Playbook and a Fundamentals of Tennis Book. I made up a forty-one (41) page playbook to show each recruit what discipline is expected from them and the organization, responsibilities, rules, and goals of the Clarion University Women's Tennis Team. As their coach, I emphasized what it takes to be a success, planned practice procedures, and set CUP Women's Tennis Team Policies, sportsmanship practices, and team goals. I also made up a forty –nine (49) page "Fundamentals of Tennis" book that covered tennis etiquette, equipment, all tennis strokes, singles and doubles drills and practice drills.

TEAM GOALS

One of the most important things to change the attitude of your team is to have written goals so your team can focus on the commitment to excellence. For example, the year before I was appointed the Head Women's Tennis Coach, their record was 0-9, and 13 out of 14 schools in the PSAC Conference. With very little scholarship aid we accomplished (4) out of five written goals. Successful people tend to think on paper. I deeply believe that writing your goals down is one of the most vital components in the goal achieving process. Brian Tracy, CEO of Brian Tracy International, who has authored many books on the psychology of achievement, said, "Studies have shown that when a goal is not written down, your chances of reaching that goal are somewhere between 3 percent and 7 percent, not very good. The moments you write the goal down, along with a simple plan to reach your goals, your chances of reaching your goals increase to as much as 70 or 80 percent."

One of the best ways to achieve your goals is to <u>set deadlines</u> for yourself. Deadlines equal maximum productivity, and all goals must be accomplished by deadlines. Setting deadlines is the single most effective way to overcome procrastination. When I was appointed Head Tennis Coach at Clarion University, I told the athletic director that in five years we would be PSAC State Champions. In four years we had the first winning tennis season in the history of Clarion University with a record of (9-4), and in the fifth year we went undefeated (13-0) and won our first PSAC State Championship.

Follow your passion – Zig Ziglar says it best about setting goals and making a decision, "You can't hit a target you cannot see, and you cannot see a target you do not have."

The most important aspect of goal achieving is that you must have a goal in place. After you have made your decision on your goals, you must ask yourself if you are willing to do whatever it takes to fulfill your dream. Ultimately, your choices and not your circumstances or situations, will determine your level of success in life, school, and work.

TEAM GOALS FOR THE CUP WOMEN'S TENNIS TEAM
1. Winning Season
2. Undefeated Season
3. P.S.A.C. State Championship
4. N. C. A. A. Qualification for Division II National Championship
5. N.C.A.A. Women's Tennis Division II National Champ

CODE OF CONDUCT —
CLARION UNIVERSITY WOMEN'S TENNIS SPORTSMANSHIP
Code of Conduct: The highest type of sportsmanship is expected from every player. Players are under an obligation to avoid acts which are

unsportsmanlike or detrimental to the game of tennis.

Any coach or person who is reading this book can set his/her own code of conduct and make sure that you and your team obeys these standards for success.

1. Loud, abusive, or profane language, racquet throwing, or hitting balls indiscriminately is prohibited.

2. Do not stall. The rules of tennis allow a maximum of 1 ½ minutes for changing ends of court on the odd games and 30 seconds between points and between games when there is no changeover.

3. Intentional waving of a racquet or arms or making distracting noises is prohibited.

4. Coaching, except during the break between the 2nd and 3rd sets, is prohibited. Spectators, including parents, friends and coaches, should not interfere with or participate in on court matters.

5. Do not attempt to make a mockery of a match, whether winning or losing.

6. Do not withdraw from a match or tournament after the draw has been made or default in a tournament, either during the course of a match or prior to its commencement, except for illness, injury or personal emergency.

Tennis Etiquette:

1. Wait until a point is over before walking behind a court where a match is in progress.

2. To retrieve a ball from another court or to return a ball to another court, wait until the players have completed a point.

3. Players should present a neat appearance and abide by local dress regulations.

ON-COURT RULES:

1. If you have any doubt as to whether a ball is out or good, you must give your opponent the benefit of the doubt and play the ball as good. You should not play a let.

2. It is your obligation to call all balls on your side, to help your opponent make calls when the opponent requests it, and to call against yourself, with the exception of a first service, any ball that you clearly see out on your opponent's side of the net.

3. Any "Out" or "Let" call must be made instantaneously. It should be made before ether an opponent has hit the return or the return has gone out of play. Otherwise, the ball continues in play.

4. Do not enlist the aid of spectators in making line calls.

5. If you call a ball out and then realize it was good, you should correct your call.

6. To avoid controversy over the score, the server should announce the set score (Example: 5-4) before starting a game and the game score (Example: 30-40) prior to serving each point.

7. If players cannot agree on the score, they may go back to the last score on which there was agreement and resume play from that point, or they may spin a racquet.

8. Foot faults are not allowed. If an opponent persists in foot-faulting after being warned not to do so, the referee should be informed.

9. Do not stall, sulk, complain, or practice poor gamesmanship.

CLARION UNIVERSITY "GOLDEN EAGLES" WOMEN'S TENNIS TEAM POLICIES

The following policies, as determined by the coaching staff and team will govern the women's tennis team. These regulations will be in effect throughout the entire season.

Please note: Any coach or person who is reading this book can make up his/her own team policies of conduct.

1. Practice:
   All practice procedures as presented by the coaches will remain the same.

2. Appearance:
    All team members (Coaches, Players, and Managers) will be expected to maintain a clean appearance and a trimmed haircut.

3. Dress:
    On the road – dress will be slacks, skirt, blouse or sweater. Failure to abide by the road dress policies will result in the player not making the trip.

4. Smoking:
    No smoking allowed. Failure to abide by this rule will be disciplined as follows:
    1st Offense: The player will be barred from competition for a one week period. However, she must attend all practices and team functions during that week.
    2nd Offense: This will result in automatic dismissal from the squad for the year.

5. Drugs:
    Immediate dismissal from the team for the year.

6. Drinking:
    Be realistic – everything in moderation. Call on self-discipline and team loyalty as you guideline. In a case of obvious intoxication, the squad member involved will be disciplined in the same manner as mentioned in article four (4).

7. Moral Behavior:
    You have a moral obligation to yourself, your family, your

teammates, the University, and the entire tennis program. Conduct unbecoming a member of our program will be subject to disciplinary action with possible expulsion from the Tennis Team.

8. Property Destruction or Stolen Articles:
   This regulation applies at home and away._
   The player or players responsible will pay for all damages and property involved. Failure to abide by this policy will result in the same disciplinary measures as mentioned in article 4.

9. Motel Regulations on the Road:
   Night before the match. All players must be in their rooms by 11:00 pm and lights out at 12:00 am. Rooms will be checked.

10. Night of match.
    All players must be in their rooms by midnight. Rooms will be checked.
    Failure to abide by this regulation will be handled as in Article 4.

All regulations are in effect immediately and each player must sign and date this Tennis Team Discipline Policies.

CLARION UNIVERSITY WOMEN'S VARSITY TENNIS PRACTICE PROCEDURES

1. Practice starts officially at 2:00 p.m. with everyone on court and ready to go.

2. Our Clarion University Women's Tennis Team practiced almost every day, rain or shine because if it rained or snowed we would have an indoor tennis practice off the wall in the indoor racquetball courts in the Tippin Gym basement. I believe that in the North East with such bad weather at times, you must practice every day if you are going to be successful and build a sport or life dynasty.

3. Taping or treatment should be done before practice begins.

4. Absence from practice:
   a. You may request to be excused from practice by the Head Coach only. Personal business should be taken care of outside of practice time.
   b. Check with the Head Coach on a medical or trainer's excuse. We want you at practice, if only to observe, unless you are bedridden, even if you are injured you are to be in attendance at practice. Treatments by the trainer should be taken care of other than practice time.
   c. Two consecutive absences, without being excused by the Tennis Coaching Staff, will result in dismissal from the squad for that year.
   d. We will not call to find you. Your responsibility is to contact me.
   Office phone: _____
   Home Phone: _____

5. All team functions start on time:
   a. Meetings
   b. Practice

c. Official team functions

d. Meals

e. Team Travel

f. We shall not wait for anyone. Lateness is unfair to your teammates and must be eliminated. If needed, disciplinary action will be taken.

g. When the team is called to the middle to start practice, or after a drill, sprint quickly to assigned area so that we do not waste any time.

h. Disciplinary team rules regarding conduct, dress, appearance, obligations, and action in case of infractions will be determined by player representatives and Head Tennis Coach when the final team is selected. Each player must sign and date this document.

i. We shall not wait for anyone. Lateness is unfair to your teammates and must be eliminated. If needed, disciplinary action will be taken.

CLARION UNIVERSITY "GOLDEN EAGLES" WOMEN'S TENNIS TEAM SUCCESS

What does it take to be a success?

Being on our tennis team does not merely imply coming to practice, wearing the uniform and taking all the little extras that come with being associated with the program. There are many important items involved with being a success, not only in tennis, but in life as well. The first of which, in the coaching staff's mind, is to not only be a taker, but be a giver. My philosophy of life is, "If you want to be happy for a lifetime you must help someone" The following questions must be asked of yourself before we begin official practice and one can easily see how important it is that they be answered in the affirmative:

1. Do you have pride?

    Do you get excited about the upcoming challenges that will confront you? You are expected to "Give me your best" all the time 100 %. This is the difference between us experiencing success or failure. When looking in a mirror will you be able to tell yourself that "I gave every effort possible toward the team with regards to morale, pride, loyalty, and all the finer points of the game." If your thoughts are positive, then pride in accomplishments exists and the "Golden Eagles" will soar high in the upcoming season.

2. Are you coachable?

    Can you accept constructive criticism without searching for an alibi or excuses? Do you have confidence in our approach to the game? Will you always do your best to improve knowing that this will make for a better team? Your job as a player is to play, not coach.

3. Are you willing to pay the price through diligent practice?

    Be punctual – not just reporting and putting in the necessary time, but working every day with the same enthusiasm and determination as is used during a tennis match. Do you come to play every day? The great athletes are the ones with one speed. If you loaf in practice, you will loaf in the tennis match.

4. Are you willing to make sacrifices?

   Conditioning is demanding; there is no easy way to get in shape. Training is exacting and the responsibilities are great with regards to yourself and the team. This may include personal denials, but it has its rewards and after all is said and done, only you will know if every effort has been put forth.

5. Do you have the ability to act under pressure?

   Can you shut out from your mind previous failures, successes, or personal insults in order to concentrate fully on the task at hand? Are you willing to be the person put on the spot in a pressure situation because you know you will get the job done for the team?

6. Do you believe in our goals, and are you willing to contribute to the team spirit?

   It is important that there be cohesiveness on the team. Team unity is a must in order to have a productive and enjoyable season. So let everyone strive to make this season the best ever. Can you accept the idea of sacrificing yourself for the sake of the team and being unselfish and knowing what has to be done? All for one and one for all if the team fails, we all fail.

7. Are you willing to study and attend class so you will successfully complete the requirements for a degree from Clarion University?

   Tennis is very important but certainly not more important than your education. You must budget your time and get the job done in the classroom and on the tennis court. Your social life must be curtailed until after the season is over. It is not an easy task, but if all things came easy, they really wouldn't be worthwhile doing. Stand tall and be proud upon graduation day – we know your parents will.

Academics:

1. You are responsible for maintaining a 2.0 or better each semester and passing at least 24 hours per year.

2. You must carry at least 12 hours per semester to be eligible to participate.

3. Before you decide to drop a class, please talk with the Head Coach. Dropping classes could cause you to become ineligible.

4. Grade forms must be signed periodically to check your progress and class attendance.

5. If you have difficulty in a particular course, let the head coach know so that a tutor can be provided.

6. Are you excited about being able to play tennis and represent Clarion University? Remember not everyone has the opportunity to play tennis. Some can't even walk. Make the best of your talents.

7. Desire, determination, dedication – are these words in your vocabulary? They are trite words to some, but never the less, there is nothing else that can take their place.

8. Do you have respect for your teammates, coaches, managers, equipment people, and everyone else who might be associated with our tennis program? Mutual respect by all – you are women who want to be treated as such – work hard, sacrifice, and execute and respect will be there. Anytime the coaching staff can be of help to you, the door is always open. If it's not, please knock.

Let's get off on the right foot and have a great year.

RESEARCH ON ADVISEMENT, RETENTION, AND GRADUATION OF STUDENT-ATHLETES

I have energetically and systematically developed very detailed implementation plans for the advisement, retention, and graduation of student-athletes. This is a result of my dedicated years of study, research, and experimentation into the science of coaching. My positive accomplishments in producing disciplined student-athletes, scholars, and excellent recruiting speak for themselves.

These procedures for advisement and retention of student-athletes were implemented when I coached the Women's Tennis Team and Men's Basketball Team at Clarion University.

1. Early attendance at the freshmen summer orientation program to assure a desired class schedule.

2. I recommended that each student-athlete take eighteen (18) hours of credit each semester to make sure they graduate in four (4) years. Sometimes you might have to drop a course, and with eighteen (18) hours per semester, this would still

keep you on schedule to graduate in four (4) years and still be eligible to participate each semester because you must pass at least twenty-four (24) hours each year.

3. Mandatory attendance at tennis and basketball study hall every Sunday and Wednesday nights from 7:00 – 9:00 P.M. both fall and spring semesters, in Carlson Library which I, personally, checked attendance. If a tennis or basketball player did not attend study hall, he/she was not permitted to practice or play in any games or tennis matches until they attended the next study hall session.

4. I was academic advisor to all varsity tennis and basketball players. As academic advisor I met with each student-athlete every two weeks to review academics and individual goals, discuss progress reports in their classes, recommend tutors if needed, and discuss any social and individual problems.

5. Every tennis player and basketball player was required to have his/her professors fill out an academic progress report every five weeks so that I had an up – to - date report on all the student-athletes progress in each class. This was very important to make sure that all the student-athletes were attending class and doing their homework each week.

6. I had an "Open Door Policy" in which student-athletes were encouraged to see or call me immediately if they had a problem. It was nice once to receive the following memo from the Assistant Athletic Director at Clarion University.

"After receiving your fall semester grades from your Varsity Tennis Program, I would like to congratulate you and your athletes for a tremendous accomplishment. Not only are your athletes outstanding players, but it is apparent that they are outstanding in the classroom as well. This is what we are all here for, to see that our student-athletes work toward their degree. Congratulations on another outstanding accomplishment for you and your program. I wish you the best with your spring season and hopefully we will get an invitation to the National NCAA Tennis Championship".

SKILL

The second most important coaching leadership quality you need for my "Triangle of Success" is the knowledge and skill set of coaching and teaching the fundamentals and skills of a sport and have the mental and physical discipline to execute the fundamentals and skills with a positive attitude under pressure. I have not met any great coach who was also a student of his/her sport and was also a great teacher.

Skill is the knowledge of and the ability to properly execute the fundamentals quickly. Be prepared. Cover every detail. One of the main goals in life is to acquire skills so that someone will hire you to do a job. To keep your job in our economy today, you must acquire more skills, and to someday get promoted you need to develop more skills. Skill is the ability to do something well, arising from talent, training, or practice. You don't have any control over your God given talent, but you have control of how much training and practice you do. Skill is the equalizer in life. Ability is what you are capable of doing. Motivation determines what you do and your attitude determines how well you do it. Skill doesn't know age. Skill is the ability to perform a task or a job. No one will ever hire you unless you have skills. For each goal you want to achieve, there is a certain skill set and competency level you must have developed in order to accomplish that goal. Skill is competent excellence in performance. As mentioned above, you need skills in sports and life for the following reasons:

"To get the job you want"
"To keep the job you want in this economy"
"To possibly get promoted someday"
"To build a sport or life dynasty"

When I was hired as the tennis coach, we had players who never played high school tennis and all players were walk-ons because we had very little scholarship aid. The skill level was very poor because the players did not know the fundamentals, the use of equipment needed to be great, and the strategies for singles and doubles. I wrote a Beginning Tennis Recreation and Fitness for Life book that covered tennis etiquette, equipment, proper warmup, all the fundamentals of tennis, and the teaching progressions on how to teach the fundamentals, practice drills, and singles and doubles strategy.

TENNIS ETIQUETTE
Good sportsmanship is the key to tennis etiquette. Use common courtesy, but don't be so courteous as to let your opponent win!

1. Greet your opponent and introduce yourself before you play.

2. Spin your racquet to decide the choice of serve and side before you walk on the court.

3. After a brief warmup (no longer than ten minutes), ask your opponent if he/she wishes to practice any serves. All practice serves should be taken by both players before any points are played.

4. The server should have two balls in his hand before he is set to serve.

5. The server must wait until the receiver is settled before serving to him. It is common courtesy to allow for another service in the event the service was questionable.

6. The server should keep score accurately, announcing the server's score first.

7. Return only balls that are good, especially on the serve. The use of hand signals should be used as much as possible, thereby limiting loss of concentration through verbalizing. Talk only when pertinent to the match, or to recognize a good play by your partner or opponent.

8. If your ball strays over to another court, don't chase it, ask for help when the person is between points. Show your appreciation with a "Thank you."

9. Return balls from an adjacent court by waiting until the play in progress has been completed, and then by tossing or rolling them to the nearest player.

10. Call a "let" when there is reasonable interference during play, such as another ball entering your court.

11. When entering and leaving the courts, walk behind the courts only when people playing are between points. Don't create mental distraction by stopping behind players and beginning a conversation. Leave no balls or debris on the court when you leave.

12. Control your mental attitude and temper.

13. Don't apologize to your partner for errors you make and don't expect apologies from him/her. You would be better off to channel your mental energies into playing tennis.

14. Make no excuses. At the conclusion of play, shake hands with your opponent and thank him for the match. Congratulate him if he won.

15. Good sportsmanship is the key to tennis etiquette. Treat others as you desire to be treated.

EQUIPMENT

In 1982, we had very little money in our tennis budget and almost all our players had wooden racquets. Our tennis clothing for practice and tennis matches was very poor for our team.

Over the course of eight years, all the players had metal or graphite racquets and had new game tennis skirts, matching polo shirts, and great sweater vests. We also purchased a racquet stringer to replace broken racquet strings. Our six courts were repaved and a new logo on our tennis wall was painted "Serve" "Attack" "Volley". I also initiated and recruited over one hundred (100) members on the Women's Tennis Booster Club who helped supply equipment for our tennis team, an opening tennis picnic at my house, and a great dinner and awards banquet at the end of each tennis season.

FUNDAMENTALS

For a coach to be successful and build a tennis dynasty, he/she must build the program from the ground up. I have outlined the nuts and bolts to build a successful program. You must have the skills to be able to teach the fundamentals of tennis so that players may execute the teaching progressions and fundamentals under pressure. I had forty-nine (49) pages in *my Beginning Tennis* book that covered the following teaching progressions and tennis fundamentals:

- Grips
- Tennis Serve
- Ready Position
- Foot work
- Forehand Drive
- Backhand Drive
- Forehand and Backhand Teaching Progressions
- Return of Serve
- The volley Stroke
- The Volley Teaching Progression
- The Topspin Lob
- Lob Teaching Progression
- Overhead Teaching Progression

- The Drop Shot
- The Teaching Progression of the Drop Shot
- Fundamental Points to Remember
- Practice Drills

SINGLES AND DOUBLES STRATEGY

I had a playbook in which I taught each tennis player the following Singles and Doubles Strategy.

- Singles Strategy:
    1. The use of the serve
    2. The use of the serve return
    3. Keeping the ball in play
    4. Keeping the ball deep
    5. When to hit cross court
    6. When to hit down the line
    7. When to hit short
    8. Approaching the net on a ground shot
        a. When to approach the net
        b. How to approach the net
        c. How to hit the approach shot
        d. Where to hit the approach shot
        e. How to react to the return
    9. Approaching the net after the serve
    10. Defending against the net rusher
        a. The use of lobs
        b. The use of passing shots
        c. How to return a serve against the net rusher
    11. When you should slice the ball

- Doubles Strategy:
  1. Doubles is a game of position
  2. The cross court rally
  3. Two partners at the net
  4. The lob in doubles
  5. Advanced doubles strategy
  6. Strategy for the serving team
  7. Strategy for the receiving team
  8. Strategy when both teams are at the net
  9. Strategy when you are at the net and your opponents are back

Every one of my players was taught the above teaching progressions of all the fundamentals of tennis, practice drills, and singles and doubles strategy to help build our tennis dynasty at Clarion University. You must be an excellent teacher and coach of the tennis fundamentals, and singles and doubles strategy because when the tennis match is on the line and it is crunch time your players must be able to execute the fundamentals and strategies under pressure.

TEAMWORK

The third leadership quality for coaching of my "Triangle to Success" is teamwork. No one can accomplish a sport or life dynasty by themselves. "Teamwork is not only essential for winning, it is a vital ingredient for effective leadership. A coach or leader is a person who allows others to reach their maximum potential, molding and blending individual strengths and weaknesses into a well–organized team or as he put it, teamwork is what wins championships not individuals" (John Wooden).

An effective leader or coach understands how to communicate the importance of teamwork. When recruiting and assembling a team, it is critical that each and every player understands the importance of teamwork. Individuals must recognize and accept that the team must always be placed first, above their own individual needs and accomplishments.

When someone on our tennis team did something great at practice for our team, I would stop practice and have the team give that person two claps to recognize there accomplishment immediately and this recognition helped develop our teamwork.

"Exemplary leaders claim that they are creating an environment where collaboration and teamwork prevail throughout, leaders create a positive climate where growth, improvement, and a commitment to excellence can thrive. Outstanding leaders understand that their role is to provide vision and purpose, to empower, to teach, to coach, and to ultimately to create synergy" (John Wooden).

FRIENDSHIP

The fourth leadership quality of coaching in my "Triangle to Success" that you need to build a sport or life dynasty is friendship. The true meaning of friendship (Psychology Today): The connotation suggests a bond between people who've made a similar commitment and who possibly therefore share a similar destiny. It implies the presence of the deepest connection of friendship, if lives lived as comrades from the distant past.

Why is friendship so important to "Building a Sport or Life Dynasty"? John Wooden of UCLA believes, "Friendship brings a spirit of goodwill that nourishes relationships within a group. It takes time and trust to develop, and you may have to work at it, but where it exists, the job of leadership is facilitated and the strength of the team greatly increased. I don't believe it's necessary or even productive to be "buddies" with those under your supervision, but how can a leader be most effective without a level of mutual respect for the camaraderie with those in the organization? Friendship between a leader and members of the team, while not always possible, is always preferable. It is facilitated when those under your supervision know they are working with you, not for you. Display genuine care and concern for all members of the team."(John Wooden)

I believe friendship is important for a team to reach their full potential because even if you don't like some of your teammates you must respect them and be able to get along with them to work together to reach all your team goals. I believe it is hard to be friends with all your teammates because many times you are competing for the same positions as a sub or starter and things happen at practice in which it could hurt your relationship with your teammates. The key to friendship is to show respect to all your teammates and treat people the same way you want to be treated and respected.

In my lifetime, I probably only have had 3 or 4 truly great friends who would stand by me in good times and bad times and have my back. I have many people in my life time that I am friends with and have either been my family friend, high school teammate, college teammate, coach-player friend, coach-coach friend, coach-faculty friend, community- committee friend, golf friend, or just a great friend in the community. Everyone needs friends and happy dollars to celebrate the positive things that happen in your life and to have someone to talk to and have compassion for you when things are difficult with your health or when relationships go south. I have accumulated many definitions of friendships over the years because I believe it is very important to have friends whenever someone else has shoved you under the bus or you have had a big disappointment or crisis in your life.

Below are some of my definitions of friendship that I hope you enjoy reading:

Friendship is the bond between two people that care for one another. They may have the same likes or dislikes, the same theories of life, and or the same values. Friendship is something special that people share. People will come into your life to stay, and some may only stay for a short time and leave footprints on your heart. Friends communicate, listen, and have a positive relationship between two people where there is trust, give and take, and understanding. Both people can depend on each other at all times. Friends are confidential; you trust them with your biggest secrets. They are dependable, reliable, and patient. Friends have fun together, are happy, tell the truth and talk about anything.

Friendship is when someone is there for you no matter what, and cares deeply for your health and safety. Friends find time for each other. Friends don't pressure you to do anything you don't want to do and they are supportive and don't judge.

Nurture your friendships. The investments you make in true friends will pay huge dividends all your life. Remember, you can't make an old friend.

There's an old saying: Friendship isn't a big thing, it's a million little things. Love at work comes alive.

Friendships involve mutual respect, trust, honesty, loyalty, support, and intimacy. You like people who like you. I believe friendship is necessary to leading a healthy life. Friendship includes someone who you can talk to outside your family. It's a person or group of people who understand who you are and understand who they are.

Without friendship you have no one to turn to when troubles arise at home, school, or work. Friends are the next best thing to family. You rely on friends for social and moral support.

Friends are the people who keep you going on a bad day. They make us laugh, smile, cry, and be angry. Most friends have similar ideas, something in common, like kindness, opinions, backgrounds, and attitudes.

A friend knows you almost as well as you know yourself and stands by you. That person will be there for you through good times and bad and have your back when the rest of the world walks out.

Everyone needs friends to survive in the competitive world of sports and life, especially if you are going to be a change agent and "Build a Sport or Life Dynasty."

CHAPTER 3

I believe that 5% of what it takes to build a sport or life dynasty has to do with fitness

FITNESS – FITNESS – FITNESS

Conditioning is the last and tenth leadership quality for my "Triangle to Success" and one of the most important to build a sport or life dynasty. There are five forms of fitness that are important to build a sport or life dynasty and they are spiritual, moral, mental, social, and physical.

When you have two outstanding teams competing against each other of equal talent and skill I believe that the team that will win most of the time is the team that has the most superior conditioning. Using my health and physical education classes, I wrote two books on fitness called *"Fitness for Life, an Individualized Approach"* and *"Fitness for Life"* which were published by Clarion University. I used these books in my Health and Physical Education Classes. I also believe that our programs for women's tennis and men's basketball were some of the best conditioning programs in the country. Our Women's

Tennis and Men's Basketball Teams won many of our matches and games because we were the best conditioned teams in the country. Our women's team would get up at 5:30 a.m. to prepare to compete in the PSAC and National NCAA Tennis Tournaments and compete all day in singles and doubles competition, sometimes until 10:00 p.m. You have to be in great physical and mental condition to be able to focus and compete for this length of time.

SPIRITUAL FITNESS

I believe there is a God. I've attended the Immaculate Conception Catholic Church almost every Sunday for the past (46) years. I pray that God will bless my wife and family. I light candles for my family, friends, and my enemies who I pray for. I also believe my life has been filled with some traumatic experiences, and if I did not have my faith, I believe I would have gone off the deep end and been a complete failure. One day when I was Assistant Basketball Coach at the University of Buffalo, I came home from a game on the road and found my wife had taken my two children, Nancy (5) and Robert (3), my dog Princess, and all the furniture except a card table and chair. She also maxed out our credit cards and emptied our banking and savings accounts. The woman took off with the art teacher at the University of Buffalo. She didn't even leave a note. That night I was devastated and I went to my local Catholic church to pray for help and I believe if I did not have my spiritual faith, I could have done something to hurt myself. I believe that everyone has challenges and crises in their lifetime, and if you don't have spiritual fitness and faith, it is very difficult to work through these crises.

I also believe that if I did not eventually meet my second wife, Beverly Jane Hey, that I would not have achieved anything. She was my savior and solid rock to help me through my tough divorce. I don't wish a divorce on my worst enemy because, especially with children involved, a divorce never ends because of holidays, birthdays, graduations, and special events.

My mother instilled the Catholic faith in my older sister, my older brother, and me. She got up every morning at about 5:30 a.m. and went to Mass, fixed breakfast for my dad, my brother and sister, and me, and then she worked all day in our family business called "The Home Makers Shop" that sold home fixtures and custom made curtains. We had very little money, but my mother and father loved each other, and I grew up in a loving Catholic Christian home in which we loved each other very much.

Welcome adversity: Adversity makes you tougher and more capable of dealing with trouble the next time it comes looking for you. Over and over I've seen the great benefit that comes to those who face adversity. Tough times make you tougher. A free ride isn't free. My divorce made me tougher to possibly handle any crisis situation.

"The ultimate measure of a man is not where he stands in moments of comfort and convenience, but where he stands at times of challenge" (Martin Luther King Jr.).

MORAL FITNESS

It is very important to have moral fitness because if you don't, and you think or wish to do immoral acts against yourself or anyone else, you are not a good role model. You could destroy your own reputation or someone that you love.

My wife Beverly has been the moral rock for our children, our grandchildren, and me. I am very blessed to have such a strong moral, faithful, loving, and caring wife who is loyal, caring, and constantly looks after my health. She has made my life fantastic. My wife is like fine wine. She keeps getting better with age. What the public is beginning to see is what I've known for forty-five (45) years of a great marriage.

MENTAL FITNESS

Mental fitness is very important in sports because if you lose your poise and mental toughness in sports, you can get a technical foul or be thrown out of the game and hurt your team very badly. You would show very poor sportsmanship and lack of self- discipline. In my 40 plus years as a player and coach, I have never gotten a technical foul nor have I been thrown out of a game. I have become totally convinced that the mark of a fine athlete is consistency. The mark of a dynasty team is consistency because there is very little room for poor performance if you are going to dominate your opponents. Consistency is not a physical problem in most cases. It is mental. Check back over your years of fine performances and failures. You will find that all of your best performances came when you were mentally confident that you were going to perform well, win or lose. Consistency results from confidence in being able to call upon you to give 100% effort whenever needed. A continued lack of aggressiveness will result in poor consistency and frustration. In other words, mental aggressiveness, a burning desire to perform well, will result in consistently fine performances, which will build a sense of pride. How does one develop, attain, and maintain consistency? The first and most important item to analyze is one's performances and why some attempts were successful and some were not. If one is honest with oneself, she/he will soon come to the realization that mental power or fitness is the key. You must force yourself to excel at all times since the mind can frequently talk you out of something that may be somewhat difficult. During the practice sessions you must work as close to your top intensity as possible on any given session. If you want to develop a sport or life dynasty you must have the mental self-discipline to keep your emotions under control and don't lose it. It is also very important in life to have mental toughness in your job or relationships with your wife or family because if you go off on your boss, you could lose your job, and if you go off on your wife, it could cause yourself to have a divorce or lose a close family member or friend. Words do matter.

In conclusion, there can only be one logical answer to progress: consistency, championship performances to dominate your opponents, and continuous mental fitness. Take pride in striving to better yourself through the adversity of pain and a lack of physical strength. Work to defeat your opponent with more raw courage, strength, and a commitment to excellence.

SOCIAL FITNESS

In sports and life you must have social fitness and be able to get along with your coach and teammates. Anyone who has been a teacher or coach knows that it only takes one person to disrupt a class or team, have no social discipline, and make everyone's life a nightmare. In life it is also very important to get along with your boss, colleagues, administrators, and the public so that you can get a job, keep your job, and some day possibly be promoted. Social fitness has a lot to do with treating people the way you want to be treated and being respectful and treating people with good manners. My mother often told me there is no excuse for poor manners.

PHYSICAL FITNESS

Physical fitness connotes freedom from disease and psychological wellness. Other components of importance are functional flexibility of the joints, good cardiovascular pulmonary reserve, reasonable co-ordination, quickness, and muscular development.

Why the Need for Physical Fitness?

Physical activity is a basic need of the human body. If you don't use it, you lose it. When movement is restricted, the degenerative process begins, muscles atrophy, range of motion or flexibility decreases, and the systems of the body become ineffective. Vigorous physical activity, as a basic human need, is vital to the improvement and maintenance of efficient and healthy bodies.

Physical fitness is a desirable state for anyone who wants to lead a zestful and productive life and realize his/her fullest potential both physically and mentally.

The goal of physical fitness for everyone is well worth the cost. Increasingly, we have become aware that the human body must be well-maintained if we are to reduce the probability of cardiovascular disease. We have become increasingly aware that good health is not only the responsibility of the medical profession, but rather, it is also an individual responsibility which each of us must assume. There is also a growing body of evidence pointing towards the conclusion that physical fitness and mental fitness are closely associated. Human beings are so inextricably linked that good or poor health of one immediately affects the other. For our general good health, both physical and mental conditioning are important. A well-trained mind and well – conditioned body is required for you to develop a sport or life dynasty.

"Fitness as a Way of Life"

One of my primary objectives as coach of the Women's Tennis and Men's Basketball Teams is to enable each student-athlete to develop a positive mental attitude toward physical fitness and look at physical fitness as a "way of life and a lifelong habit".

Keeping yourself fit is a significant key to success regardless of what your career or sport interest may be. Without your health you have nothing. It is most important that participation must be "fun" if lifelong fitness interest is to be maintained.

Rest, exercise, and proper diet must also be considered. A person who is not spiritually, morally, mentally, socially, and physically sound will never be able to become well-conditioned because he/she tears down rather than builds. Conditioning will determine if the moderation and balance must be practiced; dissipation must be eliminated. Fatigue makes cowards of us all. If I did not get my second wind and fight through the pain in my legs, I would go south and be defeated. As a freshman on the University of Buffalo Basketball team, I was 6'3" tall and weighed 177 pounds. If I did not improve my weight and strength and get bigger, faster, and stronger, I would not be able to compete on the university varsity level. I would not have been able to take the punishment and the grind of a six month basketball season over two semesters. My head coach, Dr. Leonard T. Serfustini, was a "Fitness Guru" and had his own television fitness show every week in Buffalo. His defensive philosophy of basketball was that you had to full court press man-to-man the whole game to pressure your opponent until they would crack. To play for this coach, you had to be in super shape. I went from 177 pounds to 205 pounds my senior year, and I could go through two full two-hour consecutive practices and not get tired at all because of the tough conditioning programs that coach Serfustini put us through. I am a firm believer that fatigue makes cowards of us all, and when I played and coached, I made sure that I was the most conditioned player on our team and that my teams that I coached would never lose a game or match because we were out conditioned.

When you have two outstanding teams competing against each other of equal talent and skill, I believe that the team that will win most of the time is the team that has had the most superior conditioning. I believe that our conditioning programs for women's tennis and men's basketball were some of the best conditioning programs in the country and I believe our women's tennis and men's basketball teams at Clarion University won many of our matches and games because we were the best conditioned teams in the country. Our Women's Tennis Team would get up at 5:30 a.m. in the morning to prepare to compete in PSAC and National NCAA Tennis tournaments and compete all day in singles and doubles competition, sometimes until 10:00 p.m. at night. You have to be in great physical and mental condition to be able to focus and compete for this length of time.

At every tennis practice I would have a detailed lesson plan of no more than two hours long. We would first have a five minute sportsmanship and positive attitude lesson talk that I would try to improve our team attitude and spirit. In my talks I used John Wooden's Pyramid of Success and my philosophy of "Triangle to Success" (ten 10) leadership qualities needed to be a successful coach.

At every practice and tennis match, we would do our twenty (20) flexibility and strength exercises to help prevent injuries and make sure our team was warmed up properly and ready to compete at a high level of intensity. We had very few injuries in my eight (8) years of coaching women's tennis. Our team captain, Lisa Warren, never missed a Dual Tennis Match ending her four (4) year career with a record of

(57-1). I believe one of the reasons for very few injuries of our players was because we would warm-up properly before every practice and have a team cool down workout after practice and dual matches.

CLARION UNIVERSITY
TWENTY (20) FLEXIBILITY AND STRENGTH EXERCISES

Objectives of the 20 Flexibility and Strength Exercises:
1. Apply full range of motion in performance of motor tasks.
2. Perform stretches with intensity, to lesson the chance of injury so muscles do not tear as easily as tight muscles.
3. Improve athletic potential by providing a greater range of motion in the application of muscular strength to learn to practice skills properly.
4. Enable a person to perform a skill in its entirety and with the greatest economy.
5. Promote muscle relaxation and increase metabolism throughout the muscle joints.

*These objectives can be accomplished by forcibly stretching the muscle beyond its resisting length, holding the position of maximum stretch pain for several seconds, returning the muscle to resting length, and repeating the process. Be careful that you do not stretch too hard or too fast or you may tear the muscles fibers. It is therefore essential that you build a daily flexibility program designed for gradual progression.

Flexibility Principles
1. Strive to retain proper position throughout the entire movement.
2. Focus concentration on the area of the body being stretched.
3. Stretch slowly and methodically, avoiding quick movements.

4. Continue stretching until pain is experienced.

5. Attempt to increase stretching ability in each workout period.

"The most beautiful motion is that which accomplishes the greatest result with the least amount of effort" (Plato).

The development of flexibility will bring forth this type of motion in which energy will be preserved. The onset of fatigue will be impeded and movement will become graceful.

Flexibility is a relative measure. It is specific to each joint and the ligaments, tendons and muscles acting on each joint. This implies that we should develop a working knowledge of stretching movements which affect all of the major articulations. The exercise program would then be geared to provide a balance of flexibility throughout the body.

Below is a picture of our Women's Tennis Team demonstrating one of our (20) Flexibility and Strength exercises we did every day before practice to prevent injuries.

20 Flexibility and Strength Exercises

We did these 20 flexibility and strength exercises every day for practice and games and had very few injuries to any of our players. Some of the stretching exercises described in this section are based on stretching exercises originally published in Bob Aderson's book, _Stretching._ (Bolinas, California USA, Shelter Publications Inc., 1980)

1. Standing Stretch for the Upper Body
2. Belly Slap, Toe Touch, Belly Slap, and Clap (Perform five repetitions and if anyone makes a mistake start over. You will get your team's attention immediately with everyone on the same page and disciplined.)
3. Arms and Shoulders Stretch
4. Neck Stretch
5. Bent over Stretch
6. V-Sit Stretch
7. Straight Leg, Bent Knee Stretch
8. Yoga Groin Stretch
9. Elongation Stretch
10. Pull Leg to Chest Stretch
11. The Spinal Twist Stretch
12. Legs, Feet, and Ankles Stretch
13. Standing stretch for legs and hips
14. Achilles Tendon Stretch
15. Toe Rises Stretch
16. Quad and Knee Stretch
17. Sit-ups with knees bent
18. Crunches
19. Push-ups

20. Groin and hip Stretch.

CLARION UNIVERSITY WOMEN'S VARSITY TENNIS "GOLDEN EAGLE" INDOOR PHYSICAL FITNESS PROGRAM

Objective:

The goals of this program are to enable each individual to develop the components of flexibility, cardiovascular endurance, coordination, quickness, agility, and muscular strength so that they will attain and maintain the greatest level of physical fitness for tennis so that they can dominate their opponents and we will not lose a game or match because of our mental or physical fitness.

1. Non-Resistive Phase: (10 Minutes) the goal is to stretch the body to increase your range of motion in performance of motor tasks and help prevent any injury to the body.
   (We would warm-up with the "Golden Eagle" 20 flexibility and Strength Exercises.)
2. Aerobic Phase: (25 Minutes) Goal is to improve efficiency of the heart, lungs, and circulatory system.
   A. Jumping Rope – 5 Minutes
   B. Harvard Step - 5 Minutes
   C. Run the Stairs - 5 Minutes
   D. Team Indian Run or Individual Run -10 Minutes
3. Resting Phase: (5 Minutes) Goal is to have your body recover and get your heart rate down to its resting state.
4. Strength Resistive Phase: (20 Minutes) Goal is for the improvement of muscular strength, endurance, and tonus.
   A. Calisthenics

B. Manual Resistance Exercises

C. Circuit Training on the Universal Gym

D. Free Weights

5. Motivation: The key factor to any physical fitness program is motivation and self – discipline. For anyone to reach high levels of fitness and dominate your opponent, you must set realistic goals for yourself and then work for those goals each day.

We had an eight week fitness and conditioning program every spring semester which helped our team get in great mental and physical condition. It also helped our team come together and form strong friendships and come together as a team. No team would be in better physical shape than us.

> *"The will to win is not nearly as important*
> *as the will to prepare to win"*

(If you want to build a sport or life dynasty, it takes a total commitment 24/7, 365 days a year from everyone in your tennis program. That is why in the summertime, when no one is looking, you find out if your players have a "Commitment to Excellence.")

CLARION UNIVERSITY "GOLDEN EAGLE"
WOMEN'S TENNIS SUMMER CONDITIONING PROGRAM

Objective: To ensure that all varsity women tennis candidates will report in top physical condition for the fall tennis season, I instituted this "Summer Conditioning Program".

Program: The program was adapted from the "Aerobics" program of endurance exercises, where points are assigned various activities according to type, duration, and vigorousness. The more demanding the activity, the more points awarded for participation. The goal for each tennis candidate is to earn 60 points or more per week.

Flexibility Routine: Before you exercise, you should stretch out with the "Golden Eagle" Twenty (20) Flexibility and Strength Exercises so that you are properly warmed-up and that you do not injure yourself.

How to Earn Those 60 Points a Week:
1. Tennis

1 set	2 points
2 sets	4 points
3 sets	6 points

2. Rope Skipping – Contiguous

5 minutes	2 points
10 minutes	4 points
15 minutes	6 points

3. Running

Run 1 and a half miles	6 points
Run 2 miles	8 points

Run 2 and a half miles   10 points

Run 3 miles   12 points

Suggestions for Conditioning:
1. Exercise before eating or at least 2 hours after you eat.
2. Cool off and stretch out after completing your run or exercise.
3. Walk several laps to cool down after finishing your run or exercise.

(Keep your check sheet up- to- date and turn it in at the first practice in the fall.)

Note: Every Clarion University Varsity tennis candidate should be able to run one and a half miles in under 12 minutes by the end of the summer. Everyone will be tested on the first day of practice in the fall season.

CLARION UNIVERSITY WOMEN'S VARSITY TENNIS "GOLDEN EAGLE" INDOOR TENNIS WORKOUT IN TIPPEN GYM RACQUETBALL COURTS OFF THE WALL

1. Warm-up and Stretching - 10 Minutes – 20 Flexibility and Strength Exercises
2. Volleys – Alternate forehand and backhand off the wall – 5 minutes – total number in a row
3. Forehand Drive – 5 minutes total number in a row
4. Backhand Drive – 5 minutes total number in a row
5. Half Volley – 5 minutes – Partner feeds forehand and backhand
6. Flat Serve – 5 minutes – Hit the target on the wall
7. Spin Serve – 5 minutes – Hit the target on the wal

8. Drop Shot – 5 minutes - Work on spin and touch off the wall
9. Overhead – 5 minutes – Continuous into the floor point the finger to the ball
10. Work on Power Game – Serve – Attack – Volley – 10 minutes
11. Rally with Partner – 5 minutes – Total number in a row
12. Team Volleys – 5 minutes – Total number in a row

Total workout was 70 minutes long

(This indoor tennis program was very beneficial for our tennis team because we did not have an indoor tennis facility and we could work all year long because of some bad weather in the Fall and Spring Tennis Seasons in the Northeast).

CHAPTER 4

Research on How to Build a Sport of Life Dynasty

EVALUATION – EVALUATION – EVALUATION

Definition of a Sport Dynasty:

The only requirement of a sport dynasty is that a team dominates its own level of competition. Coach Wooden, who's Bruins won seven NCAA Division I Men's Basketball titles in a row (1967-73) and 10 in 12 years, states that "Dynasties are all major to those involved. No sport is inferior and no sport is superior" Likewise, it's unfair to put down a dynasty team because it competes below the Division I level or because it's female. A dynasty is a dynasty is a dynasty. All of Wooden's great UCLA teams would have lost to teams in the NBA, but that doesn't devalue the Bruins accomplishments.Dynasties all start with Leadership.

"Leadership is the ability to influence people toward the attainment of goals." (Chapter 11 Leadership, published by Dwain Kelly)

THE PREREQUISITE FOR LEADERSHIP

"Live as though you'll die tomorrow,
learn as though you'll live forever" (Mahatma Gandhi)

The words convey a fitting sense of energy and urgency. Don't squander a single day, and seek knowledge as if you will never die. It is an instruction on how to be an enlightened leader, one who lasts. Longevity in leadership is related in part, to your love of learning and the sense of urgency you attach to it.

Leaders never stop learning. In my field of work the leader is called a coach. To excel as a coach and leader, you must be a good teacher, to excel as a teacher, coach, recruiter, or leader, you must remain a student who keeps learning and tries to improve and get better.

- There is overwhelming evidence in the literature supporting the premise that effective leaders make a difference in producing sports dynasties.

- Authors like Senge (1999), Bennis (1989), Peters and Waterman (1992), and Burns (1978), critique the important connection between leadership and team effectiveness. The evidence confirms that outstanding leaders and coaches who have developed specific leadership skills create superior performance in players.

- Excellence does not happen by chance. It springs from a foundation of personal effectiveness and efficiency that outstanding coaches not only possess but can instill in others. Individual coaches, not organizations, create a culture of excellence.

- Effective coaches can create an environment and atmosphere in which one or more individuals interact with others in a way that raises everyone to higher levels of motivation and performance. Effective coaching and leadership involves getting things done through people.

- Leadership is a skill, an attitude, but most importantly, it is a way of life. Effective coaching and leadership is built on a foundation of sound principles. Effective coaches practice these principles every day of their lives. These principles guide every action they perform both within and outside their coaching contexts. My ten (10) Principles of Leadership that I outlined and explained in this book of *How to Build a Sport or Life Dynasty* are the following: Sportsmanship, caring, persistence, enthusiasm, hard work, skill, conditioning, discipline, teamwork, and friendship are the attributes I tried to instill in my players for eight (8) years, during which time we built a Tennis Dynasty at Clarion University.

- Exemplary coaches claim that they are creating an environment wherein collaboration and teamwork prevail throughout. Coaching leaders create a positive climate where growth, improvement, and a commitment to excellence can thrive. Outstanding coaches understand that their role is to provide vision and purpose to empower, to teach, to coach, and ultimately to create synergy. The relationship between leadership and coaching performance is too powerful to ignore. Effective leadership is the catalyst that can unlock the door to success in coaching.

- Leadership and team performance are so interconnected you simply cannot have one without the other. However, lack of leadership will result in poor team performance and conversely, outstanding leadership will result in outstanding team performance. It might be true that ability or skill may win occasionally, but over time, effective leadership allows individuals and teams to perform at a level above their normal capabilities. People live day after day with unused potential. Exemplary leaders are able to unlock this door to unleash potential and transform potential into reality.

- Great coaches possess qualities that provide a commitment to building a team. These qualities separate the great coaches and leaders from the rest of the pack. There are certain fundamental qualities and attitudes that coaches should have in order to be effective team builders. (Batten, 1989)

- Effective coaches and leaders are "always looking for ways to do something better" (Lewis, 1993). This type of thinking applies to how Demming, (1986) defined two types of teams or organizations, those that are getting better and those that are dying. In organizations or teams where effective leadership is present, improvement is automatic and unstoppable.

- Effective leaders believe that leadership and learning are inseparable attributes. Leaders should constantly look for a better way.

- I was constantly looking for better ways for our tennis team to improve. I visited twenty (20) Division I, Division II, and

Division III outstanding tennis programs in the country to look at their playbook and their teaching of the fundamentals of tennis, and I attended their practices to help me to see the drills they used to teach singles and doubles fundamentals and tennis strategies. I also met with the coaches and discussed recruiting strategies.

- My philosophy is if you and your team are not improving and getting better, you are going south. If you want to improve and develop a sport or life dynasty, you must visit other successful programs in your sport and constantly read articles and books on leadership and teaching your sport.

- An effective leader and coach in Wooden's view is one who understands that "Success is only temporary." What is outstanding today has the possibility of being average tomorrow, so it is how you respond to situations and conditions that really matters.

- Success is a project that is always under construction. You must always be trying to improve to get better. Over the past forty-six (46) years, I have had every class, team, and volunteer event I've directed evaluated by the people I taught, coached, or directed.

You must have constant evaluations of everything that you do if you are going to maintain and improve on your dynasty and maintain a commitment to excellence.

TRIANGLE TO

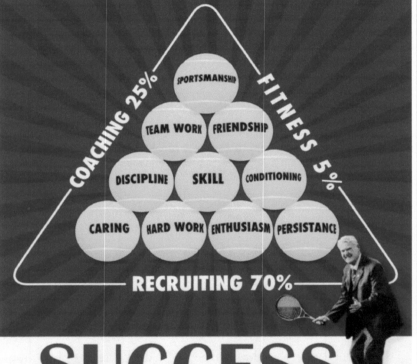

SPORTSMANSHIP

COACHING 25%

FITNESS 5%

TEAM WORK · FRIENDSHIP

DISCIPLINE · SKILL · CONDITIONING

CARING · HARD WORK · ENTHUSIASM · PERSISTANCE

RECRUITING 70%

SUCCESS

NORB BASCHNAGEL'S TRIANGLE TO SUCCESS

In addition to the Ten (10) Leadership Qualities Needed to Build a Sport or Life Dynasty, you also need recruiting skills which are 70 % of your success, Teaching and Coaching Skills which are 25% of your success, and Conditioning Skills which are 5% of your success, to beat the good teams. When each team is of equal talent the team that is in better condition will usually win.

Over the past 50 + years of teaching and coaching, I have used John Wooden's Pyramid of Success to help guide my students and student-athletes to improve their attitude and become better members of our society.

I have studied leadership for many years and my "Triangle to Success" highlights ten (10) leadership qualities needed to "build a sport or life dynasty." My own success was built on these leadership qualities and I believe they will help others build their own successes.

The foundation of my "Triangle of Success" includes the leadership qualities of <u>caring, hard work, enthusiasm, and persistence,</u> which strongly contribute to successfully <u>recruiting</u> quality student – athletes or people to make your team or organization a sport or life dynasty. If you cannot recruit great players or quality people for your team or organization, you will not be a great coach or CEO and you will not build a sport or life dynasty. Recruiting the right people is seventy (70%) of your goal to being successful in sports or life. I believe I can recruit with the best in the country and I have researched and outlined in this book the leadership skills you need to build your own dynasty in sports or life.

The left side of my "Triangle of Success" leadership qualities includes <u>caring, discipline, teamwork, and sportsmanship,</u> which strongly contribute to successful <u>coaching</u> which is twenty-five (25%) of what you need to dominate your opponents and build a sport or life dynasty.

The right side of my "Triangle of Success" leadership qualities includes <u>persistence, conditioning, friendship and sportsmanship</u>, which strongly contribute to <u>fitness.</u> Fitness is five (5%) of what it takes to have success and build a sport or life dynasty.

The center of my "Triangle to Success" is the leadership quality of <u>skill.</u> You must have skills of <u>recruiting (70%), coaching (25%), and fitness (5%)</u> to dominate your opponent and build a sport or life dynasty.

I believe all (10) "Triangle to Success" leadership qualities are important, but to go from success to significance you must give of yourself to help others to be successful.

SUCCESS TO SIGNIFICANCE

I have had Great Success over the past 50+ Years

1. Class Officer: I was the junior and senior class president at Kensington High School in Buffalo, NY. Our basketball team won the city league basketball team championship two out of four years. I earned one of the top five spots All Western New York basketball players my senior year (2 million people). I earned First team All-City Buffalo, NY my senior year and I was second team all-city my junior and sophomore years.

2. University of Buffalo basketball player. Our team was selected to play in two NCAA Division II basketball tournaments. During my senior year, the team set a school record of (19-3), an 86% winning percentage. I was NCAA Mid-East Regional All-Tournament first team choice. As a walk-on, I was selected by teammates as M.V.P. in both my freshmen and senior years.

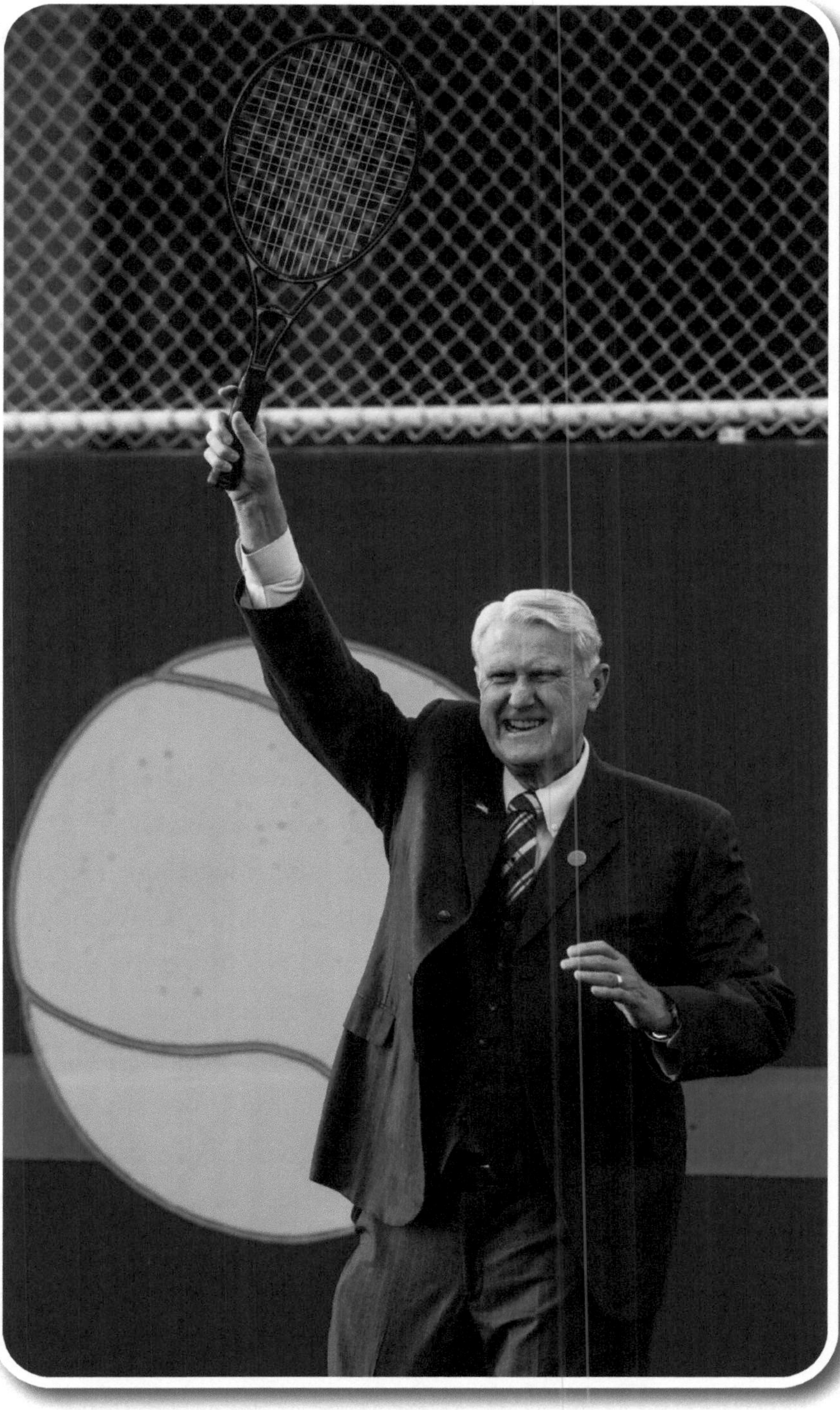

I was selected to play in the East-West Senior College All-Star Game in Erie, PA.

3. Area Head camp counselor and basketball coach at Brant Lake Camp in Brant Lake, NY. This was my first job each summer for nine years. I lived and taught many sports to over 300 campers at this all-boys 8-week sports camp. I was a counselor for (4) years and Area Head for (5) years – in charge of (12) counselors and (40) campers. I was also the boys (ages 11- 12) camp basketball coach for (9) years in which our record was (88-1) from 1961 – 1970.

4. Assistant Men's Basketball Coach seven (7) years at Division I SUNY at Buffalo in which my last year we were (16-8) with very little scholarship aid to compete in Division I. I recruited Curtis Blackmore who has his banner and number retired at the S.U.N.Y. at Buffalo and many more Division I players (1965-1973).

5. Head Men's Tennis Coach one (1) year at Division I SUNY at Buffalo in which our record was (12-4) and we were ranked 5th in the East Division I with very little scholarship aid (1974).

6. Assistant Men's Basketball Coach at Clarion University Division II eight (8) years. We averaged twenty (20) wins a year for eight years and my last year as assistant coach, we were ranked 3rd in the Country NCAA Division II (1974-1982).

7. Head Women's Tennis Coach at Clarion University eight (8) years (1982-1989). From 0-9 oblivion the year before I was appointed Head Women's Tennis Coach we developed a Tennis Dynasty with very little scholarship aid and went (57-1) my last four years; went undefeated (4) straight fall tennis seasons; won (4) straight PSAC Women's Tennis Championships

Conference record); ranked number one (1) in the East (4) straight years NCAA Division II; qualified for the National NCAA Division II Women's Tennis Championships two (2) years in a row; and finished 8th in the country in 1987 and 7th in the country in 1988; and I was selected as PSAC "Coach of the Year" in both 1988 and 1989. The best thing I did for our women's tennis team for eight (8) years is that we had (100%) graduation rate for players who played four years for me and the last eight (8) semesters our team averaged above a 3.0 and Jane Bender, our team captain, was selected as an Academic All-American with a four year academic record of (3.93).

8. For the past (46) years from (1974-2020) the best thing that I have ever done in my life other than love my wife, children and grandchildren, is I have created a "Giving Dynasty" in which I have helped raise approximately two and a half plus million dollars for the following Clarion Community organizations listed below. I have helped raise this money as a director, chairman, or volunteer committee member for the Clarion Community, Clarion University, and the State University of New York at Buffalo. These volunteer activities have given me satisfaction and happiness because I have helped someone, given my best, and have given back to my community. I have helped make the Clarion Community a better place to live and work. (The following organizations are some of the organizations that I have volunteered for, recruited members, and helped raise large amounts of money for our Clarion Community over the past forty-six (46) years).

**To go from success to significance,
you must serve your community.**

1. Immaculate Conception Church and School

   I have had a long volunteer relationship of forty-six (46) years with Immaculate Conception Church and School and have been a parish member from 1974 to present. I have served on many elected positions such as; School Board member and Parish Council member twice; Ministry Board member from 1991-1998; Parent Teacher Organization (PTO) member from 1985-2003; served as an usher for (23) years; served on many fund raising events such as initiator and Director of the first IC Golf Scramble for three years in which we raised over $18,000 dollars for the IC School. I have also volunteered to serve as Head Basketball Coach of the Boy's and Girl's I C Basketball Teams for many years. I was appointed athletic moderator for the Tri-County area by the athletic board of the Diocese of Erie from August 27, 1993-1998. I was a member of the IC Choir at Immaculate Conception Church for many years. My wife Beverly was a Social Studies Teacher at IC Elementary School for 12 years, and we both worked on many fund raising events as parents of four children who all attended IC School, grades K-8, to make sure the school would still exist and excel. My family and I donated our time, talents, and treasure, to help support and raise money for Immaculate Conception Church, School, and Catholic Charities Appeal over the past forty-six (46) years.

2. Kiwanis Club of Clarion

   I have also been a very responsible community citizen since 1985. I have been an active member of the Kiwanis Club of Clarion for thirty-five (35) years. I was inducted on October 18, 2010, into the Legion of Honor for serving the Kiwanis Club of Clarion for twenty–five (25) years of community service. I have been president of Clarion Kiwanis twice, Vice president, and currently serve as a member of the Board of Directors. I initiated and recruited twenty-five (25) new members to resurrect and be advisor of Circle "K" which is a Clarion University student organization to help Clarion Kiwanis raise money through the ALF French Fry Stand. Every year, for the past (35) years, Clarion Kiwanis members and Circle "K" members have volunteered their time by working a French Fry stand each Autumn Leaf Festival and I helped raise $5,200 dollars per year for the past thirty-five (35) years. Overall, we raised approximately $ 182,000 for Clarion Kiwanis. The Clarion Kiwanis Club and Circle 'K" have also raised approximately $70,000 by ringing the bell for the Salvation Army the past thirty-five (35) years. I have also helped the Kiwanis Club of Clarion serve approximately 140 meals for Food for Friends each year over the past thirty-five (35) years for a total of approximately 5,000 meals. I helped the Red Cross Blood Drive, sponsored by Kiwanis, and collected over 1,500 pints of blood for the Clarion County Red Cross. I often gave a double-red at each Clarion Kiwanis Red Cross Blood Drive every year. Over the past 35 years I have helped Clarion Kiwanis raise approximately $ 252,000 for the Clarion Community.

3. Clarion Area Jaycees
   - Member 1974-1982
   - Chairman of Jaycees organizing committee for sponsoring the Australian National Olympic Basketball team vs Clarion University Men's Basketball team December 8th, 1977.

- Co-Chairman of Jaycees organizing committee for hosting and sponsoring the Peruvian National Olympic Basketball Team to play Clarion University Men's Basketball Team 1976.
- I helped bring international recognition to Clarion University while at the same time raise approximately ($5,000) for Children's Hospital in Pittsburgh Pa. (1976-77).

4. The New Clarion County YMCA

On March 6, 1992, I initiated and called the first meeting of the current new Y.M.C.A. at the Clarion County courthouse and I was one of 13 founding members of the current Y.M.C.A. in Clarion County that opened in 2019. In 1992, I was elected as Chairman of the Clarion County Y.M.C.A. Organizing Committee to study the feasibility of having a Y.M.C.A. in Clarion County. I have held almost every volunteer leadership position with the current Y.M.C.A. In 2000, I received a Y.M.C.A distinguished service award for my dedication for helping bring the Y.M.C.A. to the Clarion Area, serving as the first Chairman of the Clarion County Organizing Committee, directing many fund raising events, and serving as a member of the Board of Managers for nine years. I conceived and initiated in 2000, the "Sportsmanship I" District 9 All-Star Basketball Games for the Clarion County Y.M.C.A. As Director the past 20 years of the "Sportsmanship I" All-Star Games, we have honored 760 senior players, 152 coaches, and 114 officials. The "Sportsmanship I" District 9 All-Star Games have raised over approximately $ 161,000 dollars for the new Clarion County Y.M.C.A. over the past (20) years. As a YMCA Board Member and elected chairman twice to the Sustaining Fund-Raising Committee for nine (9) years, we raised approximately

$40,000 a year and approximately $360,000 for the YMCA. In the "A New Y for the New Millennium" Capital Campaign, as a YMCA Board Manager, I helped raise over $215,000. This campaign made it possible to open the Clarion County YMCA located on Route 322 east of Clarion. Over the past twenty-seven (27) years I have helped raise over approximately $745,000 for the new Clarion County Y.M.C.A.

"Norb Baschnagel was the driving force behind the development of the present day Clarion County YMCA. In 1992, he called a meeting at the Clarion County Courthouse and was elected to chair the feasibility study for having a YMCA in Clarion County. He served on the Board of Directors for nine (9) years of hard work, fund raising, and dedication, which has culminated in the current twelve (12) million dollar YMCA in Clarion County" (Dr. Paul R. Woodburne – Acting Chair of the Promotion Committee of the Health and Physical Education Department for Clarion University).

"I must begin by saying that without Mr. Baschnagel and his expertise and effort, the Clarion County YMCA would not exist as it is today. He is one of the few who have continued to labor to improve the mind, body, and spirit of our community through the YMCA year after year. It is my opinion that no one exhibits traits of true sportsmanship more completely than Norbert. Hundreds of our area athletes have benefitted through his efforts and coaching in addition to the positive impact he has on our athletes. This effort has raised thousands of dollars of support for the YMCA in Clarion County" (Eric Funk – Chair of the Clarion County YMCA).

"I don't know of anyone employed by Clarion University, past or present, that has done more in his life time to strengthen the

Clarion Community through service and volunteering than Norb Baschnagel. One of the greatest accomplishments in the Clarion community over the last 30 years has been the final completion of the new Clarion County YMCA in January of 2019. This dream started because of Norb in the early 1990's. He called an important meeting that started the Y and served on the very first steering committee and YMCA Board of Managers. Without Norb's leadership and inspiration, the Y would have never been able to grow into what it is today. Norb also created an important fundraising initiative to help sustain the YMCA in those years called "Sportsmanship I" The District 9 High School Basketball "Sportsmanship I" All –Star Games started in the early 2000's and continue to this day. Because of Norb's leadership, the "Sportsmanship I" All –Star Games have raised over $150,000 to support the YMCA and other local charities. Although many volunteers have supported the YMCA in the past and are responsible for its successful story today, Norb was the initial spark and catalyst that got it all started. Having worked with him the past eight (8) years on "Sportsmanship I", I have not come across a person more vested in educating our youth, teaching good sportsmanship, and doing things the right way. Few, arguably, have given more back to the Clarion community and have made our community a better place to live than Norbert Baschnagel" (Jesse Kelly, Branch Director Clarion County YMCA, August 27, 2019).

"Never doubt that a small group of thoughtful citizens can change the world. Indeed it is the only thing that ever has" (Margaret Mead).

5. Clarion Fire and Hose Company #1 Building Fund Campaign Worker Building Fund Capital Campaign

I was a member of the Clarion Fire and Hose Company # 1 2002 Building Fund Capital Campaign. As a worker, I helped raise funds to renovate the Clarion Fire Hall. Each campaign worker received a list of people to contact, visit, solicit from, and follow-up with phone calls. We raised over $375,000 for the Clarion Fire and Hose Company. In 2010 I was a Clarion Fire and Hose # 1 capital campaign worker. We raised over $350,000 dollars for the fire company that year.

6. Clarion University "Golden Eagle" Overnight Basketball Camps

I wrote a book called "*Golden Eagle Basketball Camp Book.*" Co–directors of the "Golden Eagle" Basketball School Camp were Joe Degregorio, Head Basketball Coach, and me. This book outlined all the responsibilities of all counselors in our camp program. Each coach was assigned a team to coach, two defensive teaching stations, and two offensive teaching stations. We assisted at lectures, referee assignments, and one night duty.

As Co-director of our "Golden Eagle" Basketball Overnight Camp for eight (8) years, we had two weeks of camp each summer in which we averaged over two-hundred (200) campers a week and made approximately $300,000 for the Clarion University Foundation and Scholarships for the Men's Varsity Basketball Program.

7. Dr. Leonard T. Serfustini "Sportsmanship" Scholarship for the State University of New York at Buffalo

I initiated and collaborated with my Alma Mater, the State University of New York at Buffalo to appropriately honor, in a more public manner, my former UB Head Men's Basketball Coach and professor of Health, Physical Education, Recreation, and Dance, the late Dr. Leonard Serfustini. I was the chair of this committee. We raised over $53,000.

8. Clarion University Men's Basketball Golf Shambles

I initiated, directed and collaborated with Dr. Ron Righter, Head Men's Basketball Coach, to be chairman of seven (7) CUP Men's Basketball Golf Shambles at Pinecrest Country Club in which our committee raised over approximately $50,000.

9. CUP Men's Basketball Boosters Phone-A-Thon

I was a member of the Clarion University Foundation Men's Basketball Boosters Phone-a-thon in which I helped Dr. Ron Righter, Head Men's Basketball Coach, raise funds for the 2004 Men's Basketball Scholarship Endowment. My efforts and telephone calls yielded over 60% of the goal of $23,000.

10. United Way of Clarion County Golf Tournaments   Chairman

As the Annual United Way of Clarion County Golf Tournament Chairman, 1994, we raised a record of over $5,000. I was emcee and committee member in 1992 and 1993. Our committee and I raised over $ 13,000 for the 1992-94 Golf Tournaments for the United Way of Clarion County.

11. Clarion Area High School Boys' Basketball Boosters Director of 3-on-3 Tournaments

I initiated and was Director of three (3) Clarion Area High School Boys' Basketball 3-on-3 Basketball Tournaments in which our Clarion Boosters Committee raised over $18,000 for the Clarion Area Boys' Basketball Team.

12. CUP John F. Kuhn Memorial Scholarship Concert

I initiated and was chairman of the John F. Kuhn Memorial Scholarship Concert in which my daughter, Heidi Jane Baschnagel, vocal major student at the Cincinnati Conservatory of Music of Cincinnati University, performed a solo opera concert on September 10, 2000. Our committee helped raise over $5,000 for the

John F. Kuhn Clarion University Memorial Foundation Scholarship Fund.

13. CUP Clarion County American Red Cross Jump-Rope-A-Thon

    I was a member of the Clarion County American Red Cross as a board member from 1989-1993; CPR instructor for over 27 years; member of disaster and executive committees from 1991-1993; elected vice-president from 1991-1993; and was also Chairman of Jump-Rope-A-Thon Fundraiser at CUP 1992-93. This event raised over ($4,500) for the Red Cross of Clarion County to stay in existence in Clarion.

14. Clarion Boy's First AAU Basketball Team Coach

    I initiated, organized, and coached the first Clarion County Amateur Athletic Union (AAU) 15-16 Clarion Boys' Basketball (AAU) Club. We had a Board of Directors, Mission Statement, Code of Conduct, Players' Responsibilities, Parent Responsibilities, Tryouts, 15 weeks of two day practices, and five 2- day tournaments in Pittsburgh, Erie, Cleveland, and Columbus, Ohio (2004). We raised over $5,000 for new uniforms, needed fees for practice time, and five tournament registration initiation fees.

15. CUP Women's Tennis Booster's Club

    I initiated the CUP Women's Tennis Booster Club from 1983-1990 in which each year our Women's Tennis Team held a "Labor Day " car wash that included washing the inside and outside car windows. We had a Women's Tennis Team Raffle each year and I also recruited over one hundred (100) member booster club membership in which we raised over $10,500 for the Varsity Tennis Program at Clarion University from 1982 to 1990.

16. CUP Men's Basketball Booster's Club

I was a member of the Clarion University Men's Basketball Team Booster Club in which I helped recruit over one hundred (100) members. The club raised over $10,000 for the CUP Men's Basketball Team from 1974 to 1982.

17. CUP and Clarion Autumn Leaf Community Tournaments
   - I initiated, had approved, organized, planned, and directed the following Continuing Education events for Clarion University and the Clarion community. I raised $5,000 for Clarion University.
   - 10th Annual Autumn Leaf Festival Tennis Tournament (1984-1994)
   - 10th Annual Open Racquetball Tournament (1986-1996)
   - 7th Annual Spring Open Tennis Tournament (1988-1995)

18. *CUP Volunteer Women's Tennis Coach*

   I was a volunteer Women's Varsity Tennis Coach at Clarion University for seven (7) Spring Academic Semesters in which I directed an eight (8) week Winter Tennis and Fitness Conditioning Program. In this program, we worked out for two hours five (5) days a week. I also initiated a spring semester Women's Tennis Schedule of twelve (12) matches and a possible National NCAA Women's Tennis Championship. We qualified two years and finished 8th in the country in 1987 and 7th in the country in 1988. When we qualified for the NCAA National Tournament, we spent a full week in Sonoma, California and Saint Lois, Missouri, playing the other seven qualifying schools. I donated over two thousand (2000) hours of my time each spring semester to coach the CUP Women's Tennis Team because I received no release time from the Health and Physical Education Department to coach the Women's Tennis Team (1982 to 1989). This is the main reason I resigned as Head Women's Tennis Coach in 1990 because I could not justify to myself, my wife, and six (6) children all of this volunteer time with no compensation - Fourteen thousand (14,000) hours donated to Clarion University Women's Tennis Team from 1982 to 1989). In 20/20 hindsight looking back, if I did not resign at Head Women's Tennis Coach at CUP, I would have never had the time to initiate, call a meeting March 6th, 1992, and start the movement, be the first chairman, and work the past (27) years to eventually build the new $12 million dollar YMCA in Clarion County which is one of the best things to happen in Clarion County in the past thirty (30) years.

19. Volunteer for CUP and Community Events

I was chairman for three (3) years of the HPE Department United Way Fund Drive (1973, 1986, 1990); chairman of the American Heart Association 2nd Annual Jump-Rope-A-Thon (February 27, 1992); a volunteer for Special Olympics Program at Clarion University (1980- to-2010; and I was Grand Marshall of the 1991 Autumn Leaf Festival Parade as Chair of the CUP Faculty Senate. I helped raise over ten thousand dollars ($10,000) for the Clarion community.

20. Director of Fun with Fundamental Basketball Camps

I have fifty-nine (59) years of experience as a player, master teacher, author, recruiter, motivator, and superior coach with a commitment to excellence in basketball. I have directed over three hundred (300) specialty basketball schools for the Buffalo, Clarion, and Western Pennsylvania communities over the past thirty (30) years. My emphasis of these camps is on teaching the quick and proper execution of basketball fundamentals and on being considerate to others. These basketball camps are different than any other basketball camps because the most important thing we teach you at our camps is "Sportsmanship." Sportsmanship is a key element to a successful life and should be strived for in everything that you do. In 1968, I wrote my Masters Dissertation for the University of Buffalo on "*How to Direct a Successful Overnight Basketball School*". I was author of a book, "*How to Direct a Successful Basketball Day Camp*" (2003), forward by James Boeheim, Head Basketball Coach at Syracuse University. I also authored a book, "*How to Direct a Successful Little Dribblers Basketball Day Camp*" (2012,) forward by John Calipari, Head Basketball Coach at the University of Kentucky.

Over the past thirty (30) years, some of the comments from directing my "Fun with Fundamentals Basketball Camps" from campers, coaches, counselors, and parents have been:

- 2016 - "This is the best basketball camp in the country, Thank you!"
- 100% of all 2017 campers said they 'would recommend my Fun with Fundamentals Basketball Camps to others."
- 2018 - "I am thrilled that you not only teach basketball skills, but also introduce the emotional and moral attributes necessary for the development of a true athlete.
- 2019 - "The most organized, disciplined, enthusiastic, sportsmanship camp, with campers being engaged, having fun, learning new basketball skills, and improving their attitude that I have ever observed."
- "Your dedication to the game of basketball and the young players you work with is exceeded by no one!"
- "Your energy and enthusiasm will always be something I admire. It is so nice to see that rub off with your staff and campers."

- "All of your skill sessions with campers have great teaching points. Fundamental stations are the best, they listen because you expiate confidence, knowledge, love of the game, and you care about campers getting better."
- "Continues to be the best of all the local and state camps and is the best director I have ever worked with or for. The lessons are clear for all ages and he does an amazing job with all aspects. Great camp."

By operating these camps for thirty years we raised approximately $120,000 for the University of Buffalo, Western New York, Clarion University, and Western Pennsylvania Communities.

COMMUNITY FUNDRAISING

I helped raise approximately $2,534,000 for all these community organizations in my lifetime. I will continue to help raise money for our community because it makes me very happy to volunteer and give back to my community.

Special Community Service Awards

1. Named Full Professor at Clarion University in the Health and Physical Education Department –Retired after 39 years.
2. Inducted into the Clarion University Sports Hall of Fame, April 24, 2020.

Dear family, friends, CUP tennis players, basketball players and community leaders,

This letter is to thank you for your outstanding support over many years and I am blessed and humbled by your letters of recommendation for me to be inducted in the 2020 Clarion University Sports Hall of Fame. I have been retired from coaching at Clarion University for thirty (30) years (1990). My records as both Men's Basketball Assistant Coach and Head Women's Tennis Coach are well documented. Your letters and words did matter.

- " I believe Norb's motto could easily be "Excellence is not an option, it's a standard"
- "Norb is a deeply religious man who attends church regularly. He has been an active member of Immaculate Conception Church for (44) years and has also been involved with their school. Norb has been elected as a School Board member, a Parish Council member, and has coached the boys' and girls' basketball teams. He has also served as an usher for twenty-three years and was a member of the choir until it was recently disbanded"
- "Norb has also been very active in the Clarion Community for many years. He has been a member of the Kiwanis Club of Clarion for thirty-five years and was inducted into "The Legion of Honor" of the Kiwanis club for twenty-five years of community service. He has been president of Clarion Kiwanis twice and has also served as vice-president."
- "Norb also initiated the first meeting of the Clarion County YMCA and was one of the (13) founding members of the current YMCA. He was very much involved with the YMCA over the years. He was their first chairman. As chairman he organized committees, directed many fund raising events, and was a member of the Board of Directors for (9) years. I would also like to mention that during the past (44) years Norb played a significant role in helping to raise over two and a half million dollars for the Clarion Community.

- "Mr. Baschnagel was not only a great coach, he was a wonderful teacher, He treated every moment as a teachable moment, not allowing you to think you could not get better"
- "I have only had one great unforgettable coach and that coach was Norbert A. Baschnagel"
- "Norb Baschnagel is in the coaching category as "Phenomenal" and he has been a terrific coach for both men and women athletes. That, in itself, is a truly rare ability."
- "Norb's coaching resume is very impressive. He was an assistant coach to Clarion's men's varsity basketball team from 1974 to 1982. During that time the Golden Eagles had a record of 159-67 and were ranked as high as 3rd in the country. They won ten tournament championships and five Western Conference Championships. They made five consecutive NAIA playoff appearances and were district champions two years. They were an NAIA quarter finalist one year and reached Eastern Regional finals in the 1980-81 season. In the 1981-82 season they qualified for the Pennsylvania State Playoffs. The Golden Eagles qualified for the NCAA, NAIA, or PSAC tournament seven consecutive years. They produced three All-Americans, Reggie Wells-1979, Alvin Gibson-1981, and Joe Malis-1982."
- "He has a great love and passion for coaching. He is committed to being the best he can be and is willing to make the many sacrifices that is needed to be successful. Norb also has the "It" factor. He has in his DNA what it takes to be successful, not only in coaching, but also in life. People have recognized this. One individual called Norb a "Franchise Coach" and another person said "Norb is a Division I Coach that is coaching Division 2 teams."

- "Another person said that Norb Baschnagel is a "Players Coach "and he always gave you honest and sincere answers.""
- "When Norb became the Head Coach of the Women's Tennis Team in 1982, it would become apparent that he was a great coach. The year before he became head coach, the tennis team was winless. They didn't win a single match! In his eight seasons as head coach, his teams compiled a record of 72-27 dual match record and in his last four years the team had an incredible record of (57-1). From 1986-1989 the team won four straight Pennsylvania State Athletic Conference Championships and set the school's all-time number of consecutive dual match wins in a row with forty-five(45). No other Clarion team has ever achieved this. Norb had two teams qualify for the NCAA Women's Team Championships. His 1988 team finished eight and his 1989 team came in seventh. Norb was named PSAC Conference "Coach of the Year" in both 1988 and 1989 by his peers. What is remarkable about Norb's teams was that he had very little scholarship aid to offer and every girl who played for him during his eight seasons graduated. That is extremely impressive!"
- "Norb is also a student of coaching. He has written (3) sport books and is in the process of writing a (4) fourth one."
- "Anyone that knows him, would also agree that he challenged each of us to do better, and was driven to be a "Change Agent" and challenge status que," "Coach Baschnagel was not just a coach. He cared about each one of us as if we were his own daughter."
- "I witnessed firsthand "Coach B's" commitment to excellence during the greatest era of tennis in Clarion history." The thing

that has impressed me the most about Coach "B" is the utmost integrity in which he approaches all aspects of his life,"

- "Off the court, Coach Baschnagel constantly monitored our studies to guarantee that we all graduated with honors,"
- "Twelve student-athletes, who were coached and recruited by Coach Baschnagel, have subsequently been elected into the Clarion University Athletic Sports Hall of Fame for their outstanding achievements. This is a testament to his exemplary coaching and recruiting skills and shows he did what he was hired to do, in fact, he went above and beyond. Clearly it is his turn to be selected for this great honor "
- "He made an impact on the campus and community. I doubt you will find many that have made the impact on the University as Coach "B" has made. The number of lives he has touched in such a positive way as a teacher and coach, instilling values and a work ethic that has been a part of their lives is unmatched."
- "I have not come across a person more vested in educating our youth, teaching good sportsmanship, and doing things the right way. Many deserving athletes, coaches, and administrators are in the Clarion University Sports Hall of Fame because of their athletic accomplishments. Few, arguably, have given more back to the Clarion community and have made our community a better place to live than Norbert Baschnagel."

All of these great accolades, statements, and accomplishments would not have been possible without my wife, Beverly, who has given me the greatest gift of all, her love and the opportunity to share our lives together for the past forty-five years (45). She is the best thing that has ever happened to me. Without her loyalty, trust, persistent encouragement, inspiration, honesty, support, caring and love for me, I would not have accomplished anything. No one can accomplish anything alone.

I want to thank all of you again for your support, loyalty, and friendship all these years to make this induction into the CUP Sports Hall of Fame possible. Thank you.

3. Selected as the recipient of the Clarion County YMCA 2017 Western Pennsylvania "Sportsmanship I" Sportsperson of the Year Award in recognition of outstanding character, caring, and courtesy, throughout your life, April 1, 2017.

4. Inducted into the University of Buffalo Athletic Hall of Fame on October 8, 2009.

5. Received the "Legion of Honor Award" from the Kiwanis Club of Clarion. Be it known that Norbert A. Baschnagel has been a Kiwanian for a period of twenty-five (25) years as shown by the official organization records and be it future known that this member was hereby awarded distinctive recognition and has the admiration and gratitude of the club, the district, and the Kiwanian International. (October 18, 2010)

6. As president of the Clarion Kiwanis Club , I received Charter II recognition that "Norbert A. Baschnagel , President of the Kiwanis Club of Clarion, Pennsylvania is responsible for building the membership back to one of charter strength, of which you need a minimum of 25 members, and by this certificate of recognition from Kiwanis International" (December 1989).

7. Received a YMCA distinguished service award for my dedication for helping bring the YMCA to the Clarion Area,

serving as the first Chairman of the Clarion County YMCA Organizing Committee. (March 1, 2001).

8. Received a certificate of appreciation from the Greater Area Chamber of Commerce, Inc., Clarion PA for outstanding achievement as Assistant Men's Basketball Coach at Clarion University and for bringing special recognition to the Clarion Community.

9. Received a certificate of recognition from the Clarion Area Chamber of Commerce, for outstanding support and service to the Autumn Leaf Festival and to the Clarion Community.

10. Received a certificate of appreciation from the United Way of Clarion County for directing three (3) Golf Tournaments which recognized the generous volunteer service in support for raising approximately funds of $18,000 for the United Way of Clarion County. (1994)

11. Received a public relations award in 1992 from the PA. State Association for Health, Physical Education, Recreation, and Dance, Inc., for being Chairman of a jump-rope-a-thon fund-raiser at CUP (1992-1993). This event raised over $4,500 for the Red Cross of Clarion County so that they could stay in business, (December 4, 1992).

12. Received PSAC Women's Tennis Coach of the Year in both 1988 and 1989.

BIBLIOGRAPHY AND RECOMMENDED BOOKS AND ARTICLES

1. Baschnagel, N. A. "How to Direct a Successful Little Dribblers Basketball Day Camp", forward by John Calipari, Head Basketball Coach Kentucky University, Published by Dollard Publishing Company, McMurray, Pa.(2012).
2. Baschnagel, N. A. " How to Direct a Successful Basketball Day Camp", Forward by James Boeheim, Head Basketball Coach at Syracuse University, Published by Dollard Publishing Company, McMurray, Pa.,(2003).
3. Baschnagel, N. A.," Specialty Sport Schools, Camps, or Clinics", Pennsylvania journal of Health, Physical Education and Dance. (1994).
4. Baschnagel, N. A. "How to Direct a Successful Overnight Tennis Camp", Published by Clarion University. (1991).
5. Baschnagel, N. A. "Coaching a Thirty-Minute Indoor Tennis Workout" Published in the Tennis Clinic – (January-February, (1987).

6. Baschnagel, N. A. "Beginning Tennis Recreation and Fitness for Life Book", Published by Clarion University. (1983).

7. Baschnagel, N. A. "Women's Varsity Tennis Playbook" Published by Clarion University. (1982).

8. Baschnagel, N. A. "Golden Eagle Basketball Camp" Published by Clarion University, (1980).

9. Baschnagel, N.A., "Fitness Forever an Individualized Approach" Published by Clarion University, (1976).

10. Baschnagel, N. A., "Fitness for Life an Individualized Approach" Published by Clarion State College, (1974).

11. Baschnagel, N. A., "Continuity Zone Attack with a Slide Series" Scholastic Coach, (October, 1972)

12. Baschnagel, N. A., "Effect of Strenuous Physical Activity upon Reaction Time". The Research Quarterly (May, 1969)

13. Baschnagel, N. A., "How to Direct a Successful Overnight Basketball Camp": Master's Thesis at the State University of New York at Buffalo, Buffalo N.Y. (1968).

14. Collins, J., Good to Great, Harpers Publishing Inc. (2001)

15. Cooper, R. K., The Other 90%, How to Unlock Your Vast Untapped Potential for Leadership in Life. New York, Three Rivers Press. (2001)

16. Friedman, T., L., The World is flat. By Farrar, Straus, and Giroux, New York, (2006)

17. Freiling, T., A., Lincoln's Daily Treasure, by Baker Publishing Group, Mi., (2014)

18. Lynch, J., The Way of the Champion, Tuttle Publishing Co., (2006)

19. Maxwell, J., C., The Journey from Success to Significance, Thomas Nelson Book Group, Nashville, Tn., (2004)

20. Offstein, E., H., Stand Your Ground. Westport Ct. ,Greenwood Publishing Group Inc., (2006)

21 Sergiovanni, T. J., Moral Leadership, San Francisco, Josse/ Bass (1992)

22. Wooden, J. R., and Yeager, D. A Game Plan for Life: The Power of Mentoring, Bloomsberry, New York. (2011)

23. Wooden, J. R., and Jamison, S. The Essential Wooden: A Lifetime of Lessons on Leaders and Leadership. New York, McGraw-Hill. (2007)

24. Wooden, J. R., and Jamison, S. Wooden on Leadership. New York, McGraw-Hill. (2005)

25. Wooden, J. R., and Bisheff, S. John Wooden, An American Treasure. Nashville, Tn., Cumberland House. (2004)

26. Wooden, J. R., and Tobin, J. They Call Me Coach. Lincoln Wood, Ill, Contemporary Books. (1988)

27. Wooden, J. R., Practical modern Basketball. New York, Ronald Press. (1966)

28. Wren, T. J., Leaders Companion, Simon and Schuster Inc. (1995)

REFERRED PRESENTATIONS

1. Baschnagel, N. A., "How to Build a Sport Dynasty". Paper presented at the PSAHPERD 83rd Annual Convention, Seven Springs. Champion, PA.(December, 2004).

2. Baschnagel, N. A., "Building a successful athletic program through specialty schools, camps and clinics". Paper presented at the PSAHPERD 82nd Annual Convention. Host Inn, Lancaster, Pa. (November 20-23, 2003).

3. Baschnagel, N. A., "The Organization and Administration for a Big Fundraiser". Paper presented at the PSAHPERD 81st Annual Convention, Seven Springs, Champion, Pa., and (October 24-27, 2002).

4. Baschnagel, N. A., "Five Keys to Success" and "The twelve most important decisions you will make in your life". Paper presented at the PSAHPERD 81st Annual convention, Seven Springs, Champion, and Pa. (October 24-27, 2002).

5. Baschnagel, N. A., "The Organization and Administration of a Big Fundraiser". Paper presented at the 76th Annual convention of the Eastern District Association of the American Alliance for

Health, Physical Education, Recreation and Dance, at Newport, RI. (March 7-11, 2001).

6. Baschnagel, N. A., "Organization and Administration of Specialty Sport Camps". Paper presented at the 1995 Eastern District Association of the American Alliance for Health, Physical Education, Recreation and Dance Convention, Springfield, Massachusetts, (February 27th to March 4th, 1995)

7. Baschnagel, N. A., "Preseason and Post Season Conditioning for Athletes". Paper presented at the PSAHPERD 72nd Annual Convention Seven Springs, Champion, PA., and (December 2-5, 1993).

8. Baschnagel, N. A., "Organization and Administration of Specialty Camps and Clinics". Paper presented at the Slippery Rock Association for Health, Physical Education, Recreation, and Dance Mini Convention, Slippery Rock. Pa., (April 21, 1993).

9. Baschnagel, N.A., "Building a Successful Athletic Program Through Specialty Schools, Camps and Clinics". Paper presented at the PAAHPERD 71st Annual Convention, Host Inn. Lancaster, PA., (December 3-6, 1992).

10. Baschnagel, N. A.," PSAHPERD Public Relations Panel Discussions". Paper presented at the PSAHPERD 71st Annual Convention, Host Inn, Lancaster, PA., and (December 3-6, 1992).

CLARION UNIVERSITY MEN'S BASKETBALL 1974-82 FINAL RESULTS

Men's Assistant Varsity Basketball Coach: Norbert A. Baschnagel

Year	Overall Record	Home	Away	Neutral	Confer-ence	Tourna-ments	Post Season
1974-75	12-12	7-5	5-7	0-0	4-6	0-0	0-0
1975-76	19-9	8-3	6-5	4-1	7-3	3-2	1-1
1976-77	27-3*	10-0	13-2	4-1	9-1	4-0	3-2
1977-78	18-11	9-2	5-7	4-2	8-2	3-3	1-2
1978-79	22-6	10-0	9-6	3-0	9-1	6-0	1-2
1979-80	23-9	13-2	5-6	5-1	8-2	4-0	4-2
1980-81	23-6	9-1	13-3	1-2	8-2	3-1	2-2
1981-82	16-11**	10-5	5-4	1-2	5-5	4-2	0-1
Total	159-67***	76-18	61-40	22-9	58-22	27-8	12-12

**** 10 Tournament Champions in (8) years:
- 1976-77   Wooster Classic, Allegheny Tournament
- 1978-79   Clarion Tipoff Tournament, Geneseo
                   Tournament, St. Vincent- Best of Both To.
- 1979-80   Clarion Tipoff Tournament, Randolph-Macon

119

tournament
- 1980-81   Clarion Tipoff Tournament
- 1981-82   Clarion Tipoff Tournament,
  Poreco Cup Tournament

Western PA Conference Champions
N.A.I.A. Playoffs - Five Consecutive Years
NCAA Playoff   Five out of Eight Years
District 18 Champions (2) years
1980-81 Eastern Regional Finalist

1976-77 9-1   NAIA National Quarter Finalist 1 Year
1977-78 8-2 (tie)   1975-76
1978-79 9-1   1976-77   District 18 Champions
1979-80 8-2   1977-78
1980-81 8-2 (tie)   1978-79
1981-82   Pa. State Playoff
                      1979-80   District 18 Champions

- * Most Wins in School History
- ** Ranked third in the Country NCAA Division II
- *** Eight Year Record- 70% success rate total 159-67 one win shy of (20) wins a season
- **** In (8) years his teams won (10) Tournament Championships
- ***** (7) Consecutive years his teams qualified for the NCAA, NAIA, or PSAC Tour

CLARION UNIVERSITY WOMEN'S VARSITY TENNIS 1982 TO 1989 FINAL RESULTS

Head Coach Norbert A. Baschnagel

PSAC Tennis Tournament Team Scoring

Year	Team Record Dual Match	Singles Points	Doubles Points	Total Points	Final Position
1982	1-7	5	0	5	12th
1983	1-7	5	1	6	Tied for 11th
1984	4-8	5	2	7	9th
1985	*9-4	9	4	13	5th
1986	**13-0	19	8	27	***1st
1987	15-0	20	10	30	1st
1988	16-1	20	7	27	1st
1989	****13-0	****19	****12	****31	****1st

*Best Record in School History

Best Record School History First Undefeated Season in School History

***First PSAC Title in School History

**** Four consecutive PSAC titles in a row, Conference record 31 points out of a possible 36 points conference record, 6 PSAC Champs at #1, #2, #6 singles and swept the #1, #2, #3 Doubles Championship

Conference Record. Lisa Warren won four (4) straight PSAC #1 singles titles conference record. 3 out of 4 undefeated duel match season records including an astonishing 57-1 record from 1986 to 1989. Team set the school's all number of duel match wins in a row, for all sports, with 45 consecutive wins.

*****He was named PSAC "Coach of the Year by his peers in both 1988 and 1989.

Eight (8) year record – 73% success rate total 72 – 27.

GIVING DYNASTY SUMMARY OF THE FOLLOWING COMMUNITY ORGANIZATIONS

I have initiated, volunteered, recruited members, campaigned, and helped raise approximately over two and a half million dollars for Clarion University, S.U.N.Y. at Buffalo, and the Clarion Community for the past forty-six (46) years (1974-2020).

- Clarion University Men's Basketball Booster Club – ($10,000) (1974-1982)
- Clarion Area Jaycees Club – ($5,000) – (1974-1982).
- Clarion University "Golden Eagle" Basketball Overnight Camps ($300,000) (1974-1982).
- Clarion University Women's Tennis Booster Club ($10,000) (1982-1989).
- Clarion University and Clarion Autumn Leaf Festival Tennis Tournaments ($5,000) (1982-1989).
- Clarion University Volunteer Spring Semesters Women's Tennis Coach. ($100,000) (1982-1989).

- Director of Clarion County American Red-Cross Jump-rope-a-thon. ($4,500) (1989-1993).

- Grand Marshall of the 1991 Autumn Leaf Festival, as Chair of the CUP Faculty Senate, volunteer for Special Olympics (1980-2010), chairman of three (3) HPE United Way Fund Drives (1973,1986,1990) ($10,000).

- Chairman United Way of Clarion County Golf Tournaments ($13,000) (1992-1994).

- Chairman John F. Kuhn CUP Memorial Scholarship Concert ($5,000) (9/10/2000)

- Director of three (3) Clarion Area H.S. 3 on 3 basketball tournaments ($18,000) (2000-2003).

- Clarion Fire and Hose Company # 1 Building Fund Campaign Worker (2002) ($375,000) (2010) ($350,000).

- Clarion Boy's First AAU Basketball Team Coach ($5,000) (2004).

- CUP Men's Basketball Boosters Phone-A-Thon ($23,000) (2004).

- Chairman of Dr. Leonard T. Serfustini "Sportsmanship" Scholarship for the State University of New York at Buffalo (2005-present) ($53,000).

- Chairman of seven (7) Clarion University Men's Basketball golf Shambles (2005-2012)($50,000)

- Clarion Kiwanis Ring the Bell for the Salvation Army (1974-present) ($70,000).

- Clarion Kiwanis Autumn Leaf Festival French-Fry Booth (1985-present) ($182,000).

- Immaculate Conception Church, School, Catholic Charities Appeal, Light candles, (1974-present) ($100,000).

- Clarion County YMCA one of (13) founders, first chair, volunteer, fund raiser, (1992-present) (27 years fund raising) ($745,000).
- Founder of "Sportsmanship I" Clarion YMCA District 9 All-Star Basketball Games, (2000-present) ($164,000).
- Founder and Director of Fun with Fundamentals Basketball Camps, (1982-present) (38 years) ($150,000).
- Founder of future Clarion University "Sportsmanship" Women's Tennis Scholarship,

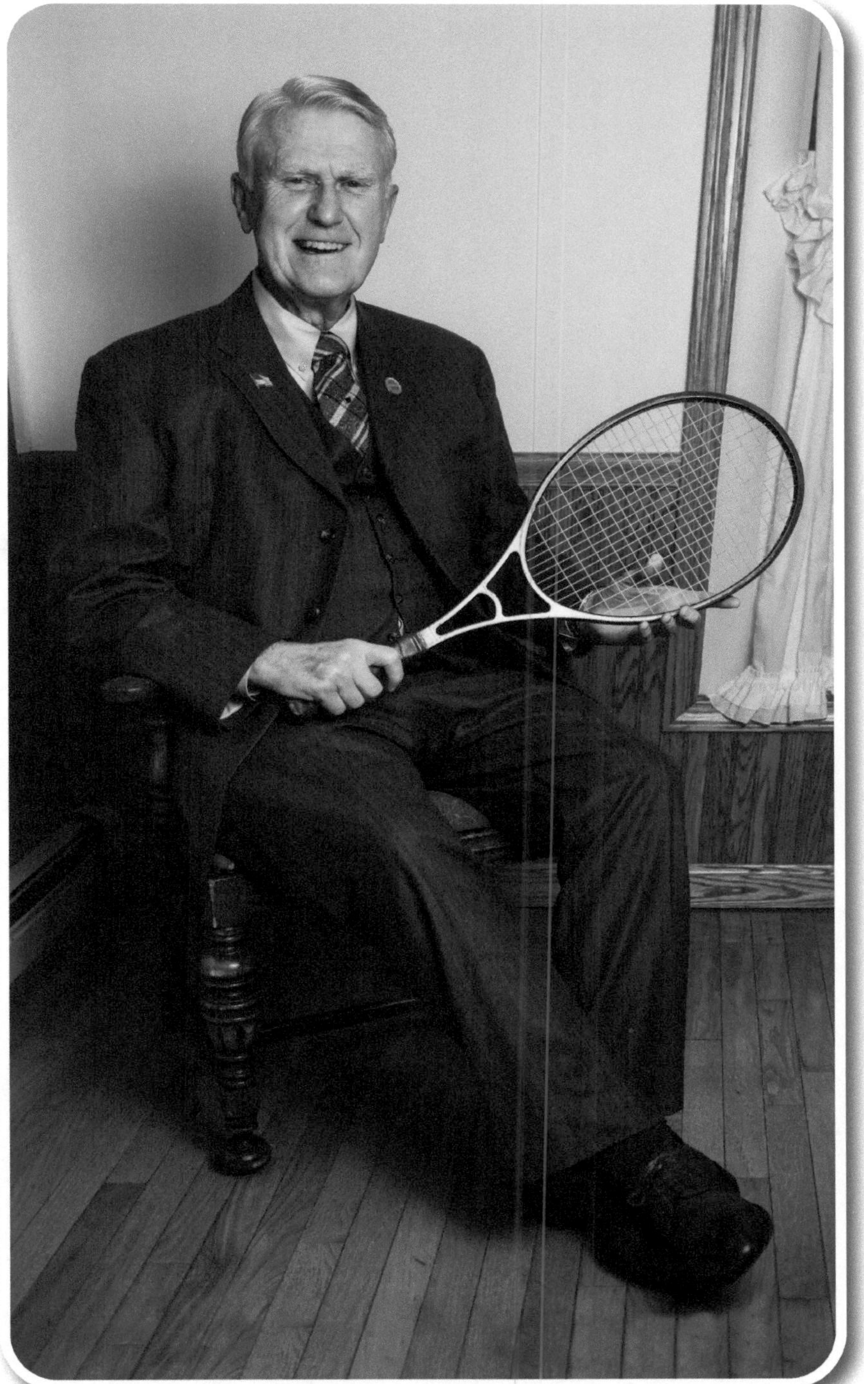

CLOSING STATEMENT

Throughout this book I have given many examples of the successes I had in coaching tennis, coaching basketball, directing basketball camps, and volunteering and raising large amounts of money for the University of Buffalo, Clarion University, the new Clarion County YMCA, Clarion Kiwanis, Immaculate Conception Church and School, and the Clarion community. If you utilize my "Triangle to Success" and the leadership qualities outlined and explained in this book like I have applied to my own teaching, coaching, and life experiences mentioned in this book, you should also be able to develop your own sport or life dynasty.

When I reach my goal of one hundred (100) years old, and still able to shoot my age in golf, and I'm sitting on my porch rocking on my swing looking back on my life, how will I feel about it? I hope I can say, "I have always given my best and I have been an honest, caring, loyal, persistent, hardworking, giving, friendly, respectful, empathetic, compassionate and serving volunteer for my family and community, and I have no regrets."

The course of your life is determined by the following, for each has the potential to change the course of your life.

1. The relationships you form
2. The decisions you make
3. The actions you take

"If you're not doing something with your life, it doesn't matter how long it is. Life does not consist of years lived, but of its usefulness. Your focus must be beyond yourself. If you are giving, loving, serving, helping, encouraging, and adding value to others, you are living a useful life. That is significance. Success is when I add value to myself. Significance is when you add value to others." (John C. Maxwell)

My six (6) best quotes to help you go from success to significance:
1. "A day lived without you doing something good for others is a day not worth living." (Mother Theresa)
2. "It's not how much we give, but how much love we put into giving." (Mother Theresa).
3. "All getting separates you from others; all giving unites you to others." (St. Francis of Assisi).
4. "What we have done for ourselves alone dies with us. What we have done for others and the world remains and is immortal." (Albert Pike).
5. "The journey is better than the Inn." (Cervantes).
6. "The more difficult the struggle, the more glorious the triumph" (Thomas Paine).

The planning, the recruiting, the teaching and learning, the goal seeking, which are the journey, surpass all else for me, including records, titles, and championships. The journey and struggle are most important for me because no one believed that we could accomplish what we did to build a tennis sport and life dynasty. The awards and acknowledgments, the final score, all have their respective place and I do not discount them, but similar to the words of Cervantes, "My joy was in giving my best and the journey."

This lithograph depicts my coaching careers of tennis and basketball at Clarion University and the organizations that I helped raise money for in the Clarion Community over the past forty-six (46) years. I was inducted into the Clarion University Sports Hall of Fame on April 24, 2020. This lithograph was created by Mary Hamilton, a local artist in Clarion, PA.

1986 Season Captains from left to right: Lynne Fye, Norbert Basch-nagel, Susan Fritz, Clarion Sports Hall of Famer

1987 Season Captains from left to right: Susan Fritz, Clarion Sports Hall of Famer, Norbert Baschnagel, Jane Bender

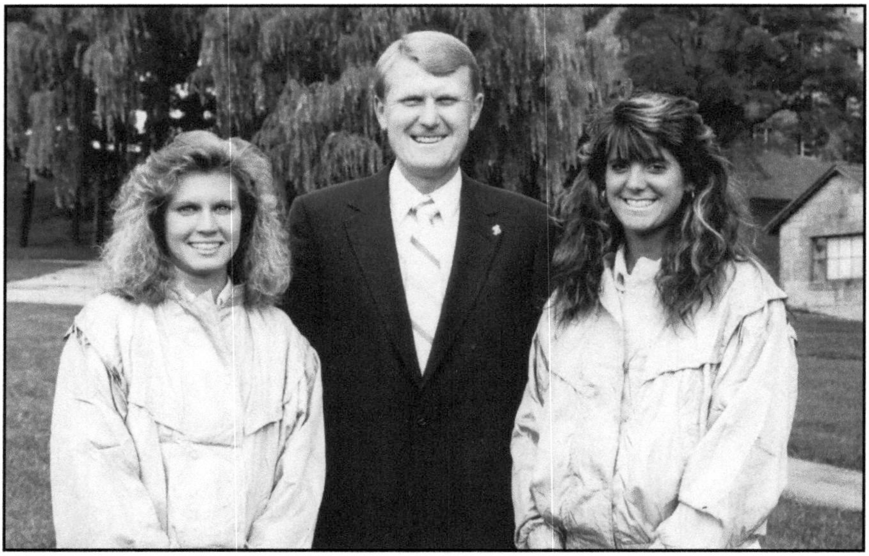

1988 Season Captains from left to right: Jane Bender, Norbert Baschnagel, Lisa Warren

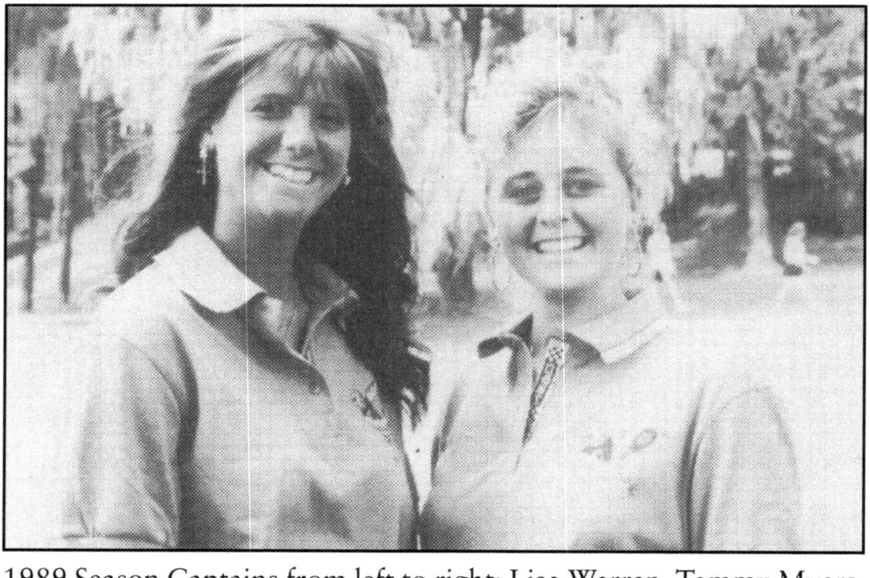

1989 Season Captains from left to right: Lisa Warren, Tammy Myers, Clarion Sports Hall of Famer

Student Assistant Coach from left to right: Phil Popielski, Norbert Baschnagel

Retired Clarion University of Pennsylvania Full-Professor HPE

Head Women's Tennis coach (1982-1990)

Assistant Men's Basketball Coach (1974-1982)

Clarion University Sports Hall of Fame (2020)

"Sportsmanship I" Sportsperson of the Year Western Pennsylvania (2017)

University of Buffalo Athletic Sports Hall of Fame (2008)

Twice PSAC Women's Tennis "Coach of the Year" (1988, 1989)